When Life
Hands You Frogs . . .

Other Books by Arlene Miller

The Best Little Grammar Book Ever!
101 Ways to Impress with Your Writing and Speaking, First Edition

Correct Me If I'm Wrong:
Getting Your Grammar, Punctuation, and Word Usage Right

The Great Grammar Cheat Sheet:
50 Grammar, Punctuation, and Word Usage Tips You Can Use Now

Beyond Worksheets: Creative Lessons for Teaching Grammar
in Middle School and High School

The Best Grammar Workbook Ever!
Grammar, Punctuation, and Usage for Ages 10 Through 110

Fifty Shades of Grammar: Scintillating and Saucy Sentences,
Syntax, and Semantics from The Grammar Diva

The Best Little Grammar Book Ever!
Speak and Write with Confidence/Avoid Common Mistakes,
Second Edition

The Best Little Grammar Workbook Ever!
Use Alone or with Its Companion Book: The Best Little Grammar Book Ever,
Second Edition

Does Your Flamingo Flamenco?
The Best Little Dictionary of Confused Words and Malapropisms

The Best Little Grammar Collection Ever!

Girls of a Feather: The Misadventures of Four College Girls (novel)

To Comma or Not To Comma: The Best Little Punctuation Book Ever!

When Life Hands You Frogs . . .

A Memoir of Daring, Delightful, Dismal, and Sometimes Dumb, Dating

Arlene Miller

bigwords101 books
Wimauma, FL

When Life Hands You Frogs: A Memoir of Daring, Delightful, Dismal, and Sometimes Dumb, Dating

Cover Design: Steven Novak, Novak Illustration
Interior Design and Formatting: Marny Parkin, ParkinCat Typography and Book Design

Publisher's Cataloging-in-Publication Data
Name: Miller, Arlene, author
Title: When Life Hands You Frogs: A Memoir of Daring, Delightful, Dismal, and Sometimes Dumb, Dating 2021 | by Arlene Miller
Description: Wimauma, FL : bigwords101 books, 2021 | Woman's Dating Memoir
Identifiers: LCCN 2021906350 | ISBN 978-0-9984165-8-8 (paperback) | ISBN 978-0-9984165-9-5 (ebook)
Subjects: Biography & Autobiography—Women | Family & Relationships—Dating
Library of Congress: HQ801-801.83
DDC: 306.73

Published by bigwords101 books, Wimauma, FL

For Jake and Shelley,
The two people I have loved the longest and the best

Save a boyfriend for a rainy day—
and another, in case it doesn't rain.
—Mae West

Contents

Chapter 1

Changing Socks

"Arlene changes men like other people change socks."

I will never forget that statement made by Joanne, one of my college friends, one Friday night. The pack—Joanne, Patty, Linda, Debbie, and Marsha—was gathered in the dorm room Linda and I shared, preparing for the three *S*'s of Friday night: Shit, Shave, and Shower, a phrase coined by Patty. After the three *S*'s ritual, some of us would go out to find a date for the following night. But Joanne and Debbie already had long-term boyfriends from before college.

One of the reasons Joanne's statement sticks in my head fifty years later is that I was shocked by it. Yes, Joanne was right; I did tend to have short relationships, which led me to hopping from one man to the next. But I always assumed it was because nothing ever worked out for me. Men just disappeared from my life. I never felt in control of my relationships. I had dated one person in high school for a short time; otherwise, I had no real love life at all until I got to college.

It is probably important to say that I went to an all-girls school in Boston. And in Boston there were lots of schools to choose from to find a man. We had the reputation of being primarily after Harvard and MIT men. I never found one for keeps, but some of my friends did.

Although we all lived in the dorms, none of my group of friends came from too far away. Joanne and Debbie, since they had long-term boyfriends from before college, went home some weekends, so they were

not part of our dating rituals. Patty and Marsha eventually found their
Harvard and MIT men, respectively. Linda found an outsider. And I kept
changing men like socks.

As I have grown older, I sometimes wonder if I didn't have more control over my life than I thought at the time. Maybe it was me, becoming
disenchanted with these men. Or maybe it was me, not willing to take a
risk and really participate because I was afraid of getting hurt—the result
of a traumatizing childhood. Maybe I just picked the wrong guys or, as
I saw it, let the wrong guys pick me. In any case, I never considered that
I had the power in my relationships—except with guys I didn't like, of
course.

I know people who have been married three, four, even five times. I
was married once. It seems so easy for some people to find spouse after
spouse. I know someone who has even written a book about multiple
marriages, being a multiple marrier herself. I didn't get married until I
was 34, and that was after a whole lot of misses. By the time I got engaged,
my parents were so thrilled they no longer cared if my fiancé was Jewish
or not.

Fast forward to today. It is now twenty years since the end of my marriage, and I have been single for longer than I was married. I have tried
and tried to find someone throughout all these years. I have taken classes,
gone to concerts, hung out in coffee shops, accepted fix-ups, and gone
online over and over again. "Your standards are too high," my daughter
says. She is probably right, but she is young (and married) with a much
more stable relationship history than I ever had.

Here is my love life during these past two decades since my marriage
ended:

- Two long (if you consider a year-and-a-half or so long) relationships,
  both right after the end of my marriage. The first was definitely one
  of those transition things. The second was very real for me, but likely
  transition for him.

- A few relationships that lasted more than a few dates, but none of them serious.

- A whole bunch of coffee shop meetings that resulted in a couple of hours of conversation each. Some of the conversations were enjoyable; others were a complete waste of time, but I have a hard time saying, "Bye, nice meeting you, but I have to go now."

- A couple of misguided attempts at returning to past loves or love interests. Those are the tough ones.

I still have not figured out how much of my relationship history has to do with my parents, but it is probably time to stop blaming them. I will likely never figure it out.

I was the only child of extremely unhappy parents. By unhappy, I mean that they were very unhappy with each other and apparently very unhappy with themselves as well. And they were just both kind of weird in their own ways. Weirder than most.

Chapter 2

My Little Pink Room

"Arlene, go get me some cigarettes."

I was trying to quietly sneak down the narrow hall to my room, passing my parents' bedroom, where I hoped my father was asleep. No such luck.

Getting him some cigarettes meant walking a few blocks to the corner variety store, George's. I did this most days of my childhood. So when I heard my father call my name, I walked into the stuffy room that reeked of years of heavy smoking, the dark mahogany furniture probably covered with a film of nicotine. As always, he was covered with that blue flannel blanket. After receiving a dollar bill, I was off to the store.

My father worked nights and slept during the day. I guess that was good, since my mother could sleep there at night. She smoked too, but not the two or three packs a day my father smoked. Didn't everyone in the sixties? Surprisingly, I never picked up the habit, although I do worry about the second-hand smoke I was exposed to now and then.

Aside from the chain smoking, my father was likely an alcoholic, although I never thought of him that way because all he drank was beer. He went into frequent rages, but I never thought of him as being drunk. He seemed to be his coherent self in his rages. Oh, and in addition to the smoking, drinking, and raging, he was a compulsive gambler.

The gambling was the cause of the frequent loud arguments between him and my mother. When they argued, I would sit quivering in my room, a small pink box in our apartment, the first floor of a triple decker in Lynn,

Massachusetts, about twelve miles north of Boston. My room was always
a mess. Because it was so small, I had no room for anything.

I would sit on my bed, reading—Nancy Drew was my favorite—until
things out in the living room got so bad, I had to go referee, sometimes
taking a pair of scissors with me for protection.

"You animal! You gambled away your paycheck again?"

"Dirty Jew! Maybe if you were different, I wouldn't do it. You're always
bellyaching!"

Yes, added to the smoking, drinking, gambling, and yelling, my father
was a racist. Although, like my mother, he was Jewish with "religious" parents, that didn't stop him from calling her a dirty Jew. Other racial epi-
thets in his vocabulary included *nigger, chink,* and *kike.*

I was never beaten, and my mother wasn't either. He did chase us from
time to time and grab us. And he threw things at the wall. Nothing like
being chased by a raging six-foot-two, skinny-but-strong man with a cigarette in his hand.

I think being an only child of parents who act like children makes
one an old soul. We feel it is our job to mediate the arguments, and we
have no one to commiserate with. For years I hoped for a brother or a
sister. Everyone at school had multiple siblings. Finally, when I was about
seven, I gave up and figured it was too late now to get a sibling. I was right.
My parents were obviously much too unhappy to have another child. But,
no, they didn't "have to get married." I was born two weeks short of ten
months after they were wed. They married by choice.

Despite the smoking, drinking, gambling, and yelling, my father did
have a job. His father owned a liquor store in Revere, another suburb of
Boston, where I was born and lived until I was two. He worked nights at
the liquor store. During the day he had time to go to the horse and dog
races, always armed with a new "system" that never worked. He toiled
pretty hard on those newspaper racing pages, folding and writing and
making notes. I don't know how hard he worked at the liquor store, or
how often, but he was always gone at night.

After work, and too late for the races, he would play cards or craps. He didn't do well at that either. And he had a bookie. Although he gambled away his paychecks on a regular basis, no one ever showed up at our door demanding money for his debts, so I guess that was a good thing.

Eventually, my grandfather sold the liquor store. And although he had bailed out my father for his entire life, he knew enough not to sell or give the store to my father, preferring to sell it to a stranger. So that was the end of that job. Preferring to work nights so he could go to the races, he took a job as a taxi driver in Boston. He continued to gamble away his paycheck, and seeing the seedier side of Boston, he became more racist.

We always rented. My father wanted to buy a small ranch house at one time, but my mother argued against it and won. She figured they would lose the house because he would gamble away the mortgage payment. My paternal grandparents, on the other hand, owned a nice house and had money.

My mother never had a job outside the home until I went to junior high school. However, I always had expensive clothes from Jordan March and Filenes, two nice department stores. I also had dance lessons, drama lessons, and later, piano lessons. Although the rent was often late, as were the other bills, the utilities were never shut off, and I didn't feel poor.

Did we have a money tree in the yard? I think my paternal grandparents were the money tree. Although not warm and fuzzy, they likely felt bad for my mother and helped out. However, they did stick up for my father much of the time.

My maternal grandparents lived near us, and I was very close to them. They lived in a third-floor apartment around the corner from us. All four of my grandparents were from the "old country," which meant Eastern Europe—all Ashkenazi Jews who came here in the early 1900s. My maternal grandfather was in the "leather business." They didn't have much money, but helped us out as much as they could, especially with my clothes and lessons, as I was their only grandchild, and they adored me as much as I adored them.

I grew up on Baker Street, which was lower middle class, but really not a bad street at all. I will never forget the beautiful lilac bush outside the living room window that smelled so good. My elementary school was a few blocks away, and Marie's, a penny candy store, was at the corner of my street. I could be found there with my best friend, Candace, every day after school, buying fireballs and licorice sticks, which were at that time actually a penny each.

I spent a lot of time playing with Candace, who lived down the street. After our visit to the candy store, we would return to my yard, playing "dock" in the puddles, or to her garage, where we had quite an intricate nursery built for our baby dolls.

Whenever I was home and my father was there, I was on edge, especially as I got older and was in junior high and high school. I was terrified of him, yet, like most daughters, I wanted him to be pleased with me. My mother wasn't much of a cleaner, so he used to take out the carpet sweeper, or later the vacuum, and I would hide in my room so he wouldn't yell at me for not vacuuming. I always felt guilty if I wasn't doing chores.

I brought that feeling of guilt—really guilt for existing—into my relationships, including my marriage. I always wanted to please everyone and didn't know how to get my needs met. And I have always been terrified of rejection. I am fortunate that I never got into an abusive relationship, since my father was emotionally abusive, even if he wasn't really physically abusive.

Going away to college saved me. I was fortunate enough to live in the dorms, even though Boston was a doable commute. And as I grew older, I grew more distant from my father: out of sight, out of mind. I did feel guilty that I had left my mother with him, but I also had some anger toward her still being with him.

As a college student and then as an adult, I became bolder in arguing with him. We always celebrated most holidays at his sister's house. One particular Chanukah, I had baked a cake and brought it to my aunt's for dessert. My father started in on me about something, and I threw the cake at him. I don't drink, smoke, or gamble. But I do have a temper. Thanks, Dad.

After I married and had children, my husband and I moved across the country with our small son and daughter, and my father eventually "disowned" us all.

I didn't have a very good father experience. I looked at my parents and didn't really know what a good relationship was supposed to look like, or how people who loved each other were supposed to act. Although I was close to and adored my maternal grandparents, they were always fighting too, although their fighting was more like squabbling.

I wasn't as close to my paternal grandparents. They eventually divorced, and my grandfather found himself a new girlfriend. I had no brothers, and my mother's brother was killed when I was 16. My father had two sisters and we did spend many holidays with his side of the family. One of his sisters was like him—volatile. His other sister was okay, but constantly complained about her husband, who was very nice; my mother would have taken him in an instant. My father also had an older brother, but he was successful and had little to do with the rest of the family. He was the black sheep, who lived in a fancier town and raised four very successful children.

So that was my father.

Chapter 3

Mom and Me

"Am I pretty?"
"You're average looking," said my mother.

That is exactly what a twelve-year-old girl wants to hear from her female role model.

While my father, awful as he was, told me I had nice legs (weird that I remember that, and weird that he said it at all) and that I was smart, my mother was telling me that I was average looking and that although I was "book smart," I didn't have any common sense.

Maybe a therapist would disagree, but I don't feel one way or the other about things my father said to me. My mother's words, however, affect me to this day. What twelve-year-old girl isn't beautiful in her own way? I had a big, bumpy Jewish nose, but I was pretty. I know that now. And I am one of the least flighty people I know; I have certainly always had common sense. Okay, what teenager has a surplus of common sense? But from the things my parents said about me, you would think I was a real troublemaker, when the fact is I was a nerd, and they should have appreciated that.

"Why can't you be more like Candace? She is so bubbly." I was quiet in school, but not so much with friends. But I wasn't like my best friend, Candace.

"Why can't you be like your friends? They listen to their mothers!" Well, Candace listened to her mother so much that when we were teenagers, she still insisted that her mother was eighteen. And the other two my mother was referring to? Their first marriages lasted about three months each.

I guess many parents say these things to their kids, but we don't forget them, or at least I didn't. And since my mother and I were very close, I really took those things to heart. And I have been careful not to say such things to my own kids. Sometimes I was successful. Sometimes not so much, especially with my son, whom I can see parts of myself in.

It was my mother and I against my father, whom she complained about constantly to me and my grandmother. The three of us were a team, going shopping and out to lunch together for years. Once I got to junior high and high school, I was a little short on friends. I was studious and very shy, so I was happy to spend these Saturdays with my mother and grandmother.

Bea, my mother, was very devoted and overprotective. She would have given me anything I wanted; however, she didn't know much about shoring up a girl's self-esteem, since she didn't have much of her own. Part of it was generational; it was the fifties and sixties. And she was very unhappy.

In addition to being unhappy, my mother was a nervous wreck. She worried about everything, and I have inherited the worry gene. My friend Candace and her "eighteen-year-old mother" lived way down the street and on the other side. My mother was always telling me that her mother didn't like me because I was "spoiled" and that her mother was anti-Semitic. It is likely both of these things were somewhat true. My mother would often talk about her mother to me inside our house. And then my mother would be concerned that Candace's mother heard her talking. Yup. We were inside the house about eight houses away and on the other side of the street. And that is just one example of her neurotic ways.

Jewish girls in my mother's generation (she was born in 1923) were supposed to marry nice Jewish boys and move to nice homes in places like Swampscott and Marblehead, two nearby towns with larger Jewish populations and more money. She constantly complained to me that she deserved to have married better and to live there with all those other women she was envious of. I am quite sure she wanted the same for me.

But I grew up in the sixties, and partly because of the opportunities she gave me, I wanted more. Because I had been exposed to dancing lessons, and drama lessons (to cure my shyness), and then piano lessons, my world was expanded. And because I was a good student and studied hard, I had plans for myself, shaky as they were.

Even though neither of my parents went to college, school was important to them. My mother could have gone to college, but it was her brother who got the chance because that's how it was then. I don't remember my parents reading or having intellectual conversations (they were too busy arguing), but they were both intelligent themselves—although emotionally immature. I never needed much prodding to do well in school, and I loved to read.

I finished third in my high school class of 434, taking the college prep courses. Thus, one would assume I would be college bound. My mother thought going to a two-year secretarial school would be a good idea, so I would have something to "fall back on" in case I didn't find that successful Jewish boy for a while.

I had other plans. I wrote a musical for my friends called *Babes in Toyland* (not very original) when I was about six. We performed it for our mothers in my living room until one of my friends started to take over, and I got mad and stormed out of the room. There is that temper, inherited from my father—and the desire to be the boss, but I don't know where that came from.

I wrote poetry all through elementary school. Then, when I was nine, I got my first transistor radio. I can still picture it. It was a beige Motorola with a big round, silver speaker on the front, and it was attached to my ear for many years to come. In junior high, I began to write songs, mostly lyrics, but I knew how to write music from my piano lessons, so some of my songs also had written-out melodies. I decided I wanted to be a songwriter, and my high school yearbook states just that.

Because of my love of pop music, I was a regular reader of *Billboard Magazine.* I thought songwriting might be a little difficult to break into, and I had always loved to write, so perhaps I could get a job writing for *Billboard* or some other music magazine. I decided I wanted to go to college in New York City, where I could be a songwriter or write for a music magazine.

I also thought about being an actress. I sent away for information from acting schools, including the acting department at the University of Southern California.

But where were my parents going to get the money for college, when they sometimes didn't have money for the rent? I figured I could get scholarships or loans. In any case, it wouldn't hurt to apply to good schools. My high school counselor certainly expected me to go to college.

Some people have parents who tell them they can be anything they set their minds to if they work hard enough. Parents like that probably were rarer in my generation, but I think some people had them. I didn't. Especially my mother. She told me I couldn't be an actress. Life wasn't limitless for me. But despite my mother, I didn't do too badly—eventually. It took a long, long time for me to reach what I consider to be anywhere near my "potential."

I wanted to go to a girl's college because I was under the questionable assumption that it would be easier to meet men there. My first choice was Barnard, Columbia's sister school, because it was in New York City, and it was ivy league. I also applied to Connecticut College, another girls school. And Simmons College (now Simmons University), yet another girls school in Boston. My safe school was University of Massachusetts.

My parents took me to all three girls schools for interviews. After my interview at Barnard, my father said I could not go to school in that neighborhood (Harlem). At Connecticut College, all the girls had straight, shiny dark hair and eyeliner, and appeared to be rather snooty. I didn't think I would fit in there. I don't remember interviewing at Simmons, but I know I must have. It had a good reputation and one of my cousins was just graduating from there. Simmons also had a journalism program, which the other schools did not.

I was accepted at all three girls schools with scholarships. I often regret that I didn't choose Barnard, although my life would have gone in a completely different direction, and I wouldn't have had the children I had, so that is always something to consider when you have regrets. I chickened out of going to Barnard. I was afraid, I guess, to go that far away. I was shy, and I was too weak to stand up to what my parents thought. I also felt Simmons might be better for me because they had a journalism program, whereas at Barnard I would have had to major in English literature.

I eventually became a strong woman, but it took a long time, and I wasn't strong enough then to stick up for myself and what I wanted, which originally was to be an actress or songwriter.

My mother said a lot of things that made me feel bad about myself—and then bad about my relationships with boys when I was growing up. After the childhood I had, it is a wonder I ever had a date at all.

Going away to college saved me. I can't imagine what would have become of me if I had continued to live at home.

Chapter 4

Remember When We Weren't Self-Conscious?

"Arlene and Jimmy sitting in a tree, K-I-S-S-I-N-G."

My first love was Jimmy (James) Andrews, and although my friend Candace sang those words to me, she too had a crush on him. James was very cute.

This "love life" of mine began when I was about seven and in first grade. That is the first time I remember "being in love," which I suppose was a crush, or "puppy love." The odd thing is that I was most popular when I was in elementary school. By *popular,* I mean that the boys I liked, liked me back, and I wasn't always driving myself crazy thinking about what I was doing right or wrong and wondering if they liked me—as I have done ever since elementary school.

Sitting in a Tree (1958)

James, as he preferred to be called, lived on the corner of my street at the opposite end of where I lived. Candace lived nearer to James. His house was the nicest on the street because he was the minister's son, and the house was made for the local Episcopalian minister to live in. Candace actually went to that church, so she had an "in" with James. But then, the year before, I had gone to kindergarten with James. His parents had sent him to the Jewish Community Center kindergarten. This was when kindergarten was private and not part of the public school system.

I think he liked us both, but not at the same time. I remember he had a big tree in his front yard where we sat for my first kiss. And I didn't ruminate over how he felt about me. I didn't even get jealous because there was another girl involved. Neither Candace nor I were anything more than friends with James—after all, we were pretty young—and he moved away long before we got to junior high school.

Dance Partners (1960)

My second "love" appeared when I was in third grade. That was when Tom Falco and his family moved into the third-floor apartment in the triple decker where I lived until I went to college. Like James, Tom was also very cute. There was no father there, just his mother and a sister. His mother, Louise, was very loud. She really wasn't "our kind of people," my mother would say, although they had to eventually become somewhat friendly.

I had started taking dance lessons in first grade, semi-private lessons with my best friend, Candace. After a year, I started taking private lessons in Alice MacDonald's garage in Saugus, the next town over. It wasn't fancy, but Alice was a really good teacher, especially in tap, which was my favorite. These days, hardly anyone takes private dance lessons, but we did back then. I took tap, ballet, and jazz.

But back to Tom. He and I were the same age, so we started playing together. His mother worked outside the home and sometimes needed my mother to watch her kids for a while after school. Louise knew that I took dance lessons and thought it would be cute if Tom and I took ballroom dance lessons together. I don't know if our mothers realized we were already in a "romantic" relationship, and that Tom liked me enough to want to dance with a girl! And Tom was no wuss; he was a Dennis the Menace type, with a sly smile. He had a real way with the ladies; he would point to his lips, and then we would kiss. Romance of the eight-year-olds.

My mother asked Alice if she could teach us ballroom dance. So we learned the cha-cha. And we were pretty darn good. I still have a photo of us dancing together in a recital.

Who knows what would have happened between us if Tom hadn't moved away.

Squirt Gun Flirting (1961)

Judging from my fifth-grade school photo, I was at an awkward stage. My nose had grown overnight, and my hair was, let's just say, not in its most flattering style.

But Scott Patterson and Robert Contos didn't care. They were close friends, and some of the kids in school told me that both boys "liked" me. These relationships were strictly platonic. Everyone in my elementary school pretty much lived within easy walking distance of everyone else. Every day after school, Scott and Robert would come over to my house with water guns. It was just the three of us, and I liked both boys equally. I didn't think about my nose or if my hair looked okay; I just had fun.

Besides playing with water guns—"squirt guns" as we called them—Scott and Robert introduced me to the *The Hardy Boys* series of books, which I enjoyed almost as much as Nancy Drew. The happy trio eventually faded away, but the two boys remained my friends throughout junior high and high school, especially Scott. When I went to my fiftieth (yikes!!!!) high school reunion, they were both there with their wives. I don't think we said one word to each other. I wonder if they remember the water gun fights as well as I do.

Mom and me

My maternal grandmother—
my favorite person

Dancing with Tom Falco—
eight years old

My very awkward
fifth grade photo

Improved at age thirteen

Chapter 5

The Prom Years

"Marc called and told me he can't go to the prom with me.
Something about his cousin in Calgary, and the family has to go see him."

"Oh, that sounds like an excuse.
He probably just doesn't want to go to the prom with you,"
my mother replied.

That was the senior prom. So that is how my later teens went with my mom.

It wasn't as if I didn't prep well for my teenage years. It was around fifth or sixth grade when Candace and I started reading *Seventeen Magazine* and pretending we were the models. I started using Cutex pink lipstick. Real boys our age were not very interesting, so we started pretending that the pop idols of the times were our brothers. Looking back, I don't know why we didn't make them our boyfriends rather than our brothers!

I think Candace had about twenty such "brothers." I date myself by naming these guys, but if you were born in the fifties, you will know whom I am talking about: Paul Anka (my then favorite), Bobby Vinton, Bobby Rydell, Fabian (Candace's favorite), Gene Pitney, and several others. We felt good about ourselves and thought we were pretty cute.

It was when I was in junior high and high school that my mother started doing a real number on me. During high school, she looked at me and said, "I am so glad you are getting your nose fixed soon."

Funny how James and Tom and Scott and Robert didn't care about my nose. And I guess neither did I back then. I did have it "fixed" when

I was a senior in high school. Did it change my social life? Probably not. Did it improve my self-confidence? Probably, but I should have had self-confidence with a bump on my nose. I had a lot going for me. Would I do it again if I were in high school now? Probably, but I think my face lost something when I lost that big bump on my nose. I actually fixed it twice more when I was much older and married with two babies. I rarely think about my nose anymore, and many people have told me they like my profile. I still don't most of the time. But now I have wrinkles and other things to think about!

The Boy Your Mother Likes (1963)

Ever have one of those boys hanging around that your mother just loves, but you think is weird? I had more than one of those, and the first one was in elementary school, although we went through junior high and high school together too. Bruce Goldberg was a very nice boy. Some of us local Jewish kids used to go to ballroom dances at the synagogue when we were in fifth and sixth grades, and Bruce would always ask me to dance. I said yes, but I am quite sure I never wanted to dance with him. We never dated or went to anything together, but my mother would always remark what a nice boy Bruce was, and why didn't I like him—and why didn't I like anyone who was nice? Well, Bruce wore his pants up to his neck for one thing. And he had big Coke-bottle glasses. He was just too nerdy for a sophisticated twelve-year-old like me. Back then, there were no cool nerds. Now, I am a nerd myself and proud of it. I don't know what ever happened to Bruce. Maybe he is cool now.

Junior High Prom: The Bet (1966)

With all my "loves" in elementary school, junior high was another story. I guess junior high is no skate in the park for most kids. For me, it was not a very social time. I spent most of my non-school time studying, reading, and obsessively listening to music.

"Hey, someone bet Max five dollars that he wouldn't ask you the prom."

Max was not my boyfriend in ninth grade. He was just a classmate I sometimes socialized with in a group. We were two of the half dozen or so Jewish students at school, so we probably hung out at synagogue one or twice a year too.

I don't know if there was actually a bet, but my invitation to the prom came from Max in the form of a note on a scrap of paper during English class.

I am not sure who told me about this bet, but it could have been Dennis Rylan, a mean kid who made fun of my nose. Of course, at one time I had a crush on him, a bad boy. It might have been my mother who told me, although I am not sure if she was in the junior high rumor circuit. She did seem to assume that no one would want to go anywhere with me.

Max and I did go to the prom. And we went out for Chinese food afterwards with a group of people. And now, a zillion years later, we are friends.

My fortieth high school reunion was about ten years ago. At that time I lived in California, clear across the country from my reunion. Since I didn't consider high school among my finer moments, I didn't consider spending the money to go to this reunion. I had gone only to my twentieth reunion, with my husband, when I still lived close by in Massachusetts and when I was still married.

Even though I didn't go to that reunion, I connected with many of my classmates over Facebook at that time. These people weren't even friends in school, but merely acquaintances. But we have gotten to be friends over Facebook. They have supported me throughout my writing career and bought my books. And I did go the recent fiftieth reunion, since I had moved back to the East Coast, and well—it was the fiftieth after all! Several of my classmates now live in Florida, where I now live. One lives pretty close to me and is now one of my best friends.

Max is one of the friends I reconnected with on Facebook. We have spoken on the phone many times. He never married, but he has been with the same woman for several decades. He ended up being a teacher and is a really good guy. Unlike me, he actually remembers the prom. And he says we went out other times as well, even though I don't remember that—probably with other school friends.

About ten years ago, when I lived in California and went back to the East Coast to see my daughter, Max showed me around our old stomping grounds and how they have changed. And we ate lunch at the very same restaurant where we went after the prom. I couldn't believe it was still in business so many decades later.

Stood Up (1969)

I met Marc Bartol at a New Year's Eve party during my senior year in high school. He was a college student and my first actual "relationship." Although the relationship, if you can call it that, lasted until sometime in July, I don't think we went out more than seven or eight times. Our dating finale was a Blood, Sweat, and Tears concert, which was pretty cool.

My friend Candace said I was so lucky to have a great date to see this concert—and a special outfit I bought for the event. I can still picture it. It was silky bright blue pants and a red, white, and blue print sleeveless top. It was almost like loungewear it was so comfortable, and I ended up wearing it to death.

I digress, but it wasn't unusual for me to wear loungewear or other "inappropriate" clothes. After college, I had a lime green short nightgown that I used to wear on dates. I thought at the time that it looked like a dress, and no one ever said anything about it looking like a nightgown. And then I once wore a long strapless sundress to a job interview right after I graduated from college. I didn't get the job. I thought I looked nice. But then I am the same straight-A student who wore a skirt to high school that was so short that the very strict assistant principal asked me if I was going to wear my bathing suit the next day.

Back to Marc. Since we were dating at the time of my senior prom, I asked him to go, and he accepted. Then, a while later—but not last minute—he told me he couldn't go. He said he had to go see his cousin in

Calgary. All I knew about Calgary was that it was in Canada, so of course I looked it up on a map. I am not sure if someone was sick or had died or what.

Enter my mother, who said it was probably just an excuse, and he just didn't want to go to the prom with me. This was about the time she started harping on "chasing boys," and if I chased them, they wouldn't want me. I couldn't give you an example of me chasing any boy (back then, anyway), but the warning is still firmly etched in my mind. It is the reason I cannot tolerate cat-and-mouse games in relationships, and why at my age I still never know what I am doing.

The Blood, Sweat, and Tears concert was in July, so I did see Marc after the prom to which I did not go. There was no official breakup, just his disappearance after we went to that concert. Although I was still a virgin (and would be so for a couple more years), I got the feeling I wasn't prudish enough for him. Maybe my mother said something to make me feel that way when he never called again.

Chapter 6

College: Girls, Girls, Girls

"Dad, I can't sleep here. I need some pills."

My diminutive college roommate was settled in bed with her big art history textbook. As usual. A few minutes earlier, she had been on the phone with her father, who was a doctor, once again yelling that she needed pills to sleep.

Back in the day, they called girls like my freshman college roommate, Karine, JAPS, or Jewish American Princesses. That label, probably politically incorrect now, fit her perfectly. She was from New York and never seemed happy with our school in Boston. After freshman year, she transferred somewhere.

We never became friends, although at the end of freshman year, we did become a bit friendlier. For just about the entire freshman year, I was out of the room whenever possible and had made my group of friends from other women on our dorm floor.

At the end of our freshman orientation week, there was a mixer (a dance) to introduce us to the nearby boys, mainly students from Harvard and MIT, our primary husband targets. And I am quite sure some of the women met their future husbands that very night. I met a very nice boy, handsome too. His name was David Packer, a Harvard freshman. I never heard from him after that evening, although I thought I might. Was that an omen of what was to become of my love life?

Do I regret going to an all-girls college? Absolutely! I would never do that again, and I would never recommend it to anyone. The school I went to, Simmons, is still all girls in the undergraduate portion. The idea was—and I assume still is—that girls do better in classes with all girls; they are able to be themselves and are less intimidated. How dated that premise seems now. I firmly believe that if I had been in classes with boys, I would have met someone and married him. I really believe that. Going to an all-girls school was a bad decision, at least for me.

I don't know if I changed men like other women change socks, but I did date an array of men in college. However, nothing really stuck, so it wasn't always a whole lot of fun. A few of these men stood out—either because of the length of the relationship or its absurdity.

The Elephant Pants (1970)

"That's a really nice outfit. I like the scarf."

"Yeah, thanks. I got it all today at George's Folly on Coolidge Corner."

I met Jeff Ehrenberg at a New Year's Eve party during my freshman year. He was kind of cute, and how many guys buy a special outfit for a party? He was wearing maroon bellbottoms—remember, this was the seventies—a denim shirt, and a maroon and blue scarf. He looked really put together.

I looked pretty spiffy myself. I was wearing what I think were called elephant pants. They were wide-legged, very bright pink-and-white-plaid pants with a bib and suspenders. I had on a stretchy, tight, white long-sleeved shirt with them. I always liked to draw attention to myself with my clothes.

We talked for a while, and then we made out—right there in public—and that was the beginning of our "relationship." I put the word *relationship* in quotes because it went on for over three years but was never apparently serious. For most of the time, it was a long-distance relationship; Jeff was a year ahead of me in college and was home for the holiday break when we met. He was in school in Maine, while I was in

Boston. There was no texting or e-mailing then, so we started writing to each other. He was an English literature major and his letters were poetic, always beginning with "My Faire Damsel." We wrote about once a week and rarely talked on the phone.

We saw each other during college breaks and summers. But we never saw too much of each other, which irked me no end. I might see him once during a two-week break. I used to wait and wait by the phone hoping he would call. I was always thrilled when he asked me to go somewhere. Many times it was to a party or gathering with two couples he was friendly with. These were real couples, who saw each other regularly. I never knew why we had the type of relationship we did, and I went out with other people during those three years, which was practically my entire time in college, minus the first semester of my freshman year and some of the last semester of my senior year. I assume he did as well, but we never talked about it.

One highlight of our time together was visiting his friend in college in Worcester, Massachusetts, so Jeff must have come home for the weekend. We slept on a sofa in the lobby of the dorm, and I was too young and in love to care that students were walking in and out all night. That was the night that Jeff told me I had the body of a Playboy bunny. It was a nice compliment at the time and one that I apparently will never forget.

Although we didn't see each other often, we were close enough that when his father had a major emergency health crisis, he called me to go to the hospital with him. And a couple of years later, when my mother had surgery, he was there with me as well.

In the early spring of my senior year, we broke up. Jeff had graduated from college and was now in graduate school, still in Maine. He had started calling me at 10 p.m. for some reason, a little late to my liking. And by that time, I had begun seeing someone else whom I was absolutely nuts about. So, I started avoiding Jeff's 10 p.m. calls.

Shortly after I began to avoid his calls, he must have figured something was up. We broke up in a phone call that I did answer. It was a simple breakup. I told him I had found someone else who was more engaged with me. His response was, "I enjoyed going out with you." That was how we broke up after three years. He was always nice, if neglectful.

Jeff and I reconnected on social media years ago. We had lunch about nine or ten years ago when I went to Boston to see my daughter. It was the same trip to Boston in which I got together with Max, my ninth-grade prom date. Like Max, Jeff has never married. I often wonder why so many men I dated never married or married late. However, he, like Max, did find someone whom he has been with for many years now.

While I was having that lunch with Jeff a decade ago, I was thinking that I now understood why we never really meshed as a couple. And I was really glad it didn't work out between us. By the time we reunited, we had really grown apart from the people we were in college. But still, he is a nice guy.

My Harvard Man (1972)

My mother answered the door when Paul arrived all the way from Mattapan to see me in Lynn, which required three bus rides. She was very impressed he would do all that to see me for a day at the beach.

I met Paul Berman sophomore year. He was a Harvard student, not very attractive, looking back, but he appealed to me at the time. I was really into him for a while, and he was ambivalent. After a few months, the relationship waned, and he faded from view. I went on to another "pair of socks."

Toward the end of sophomore year, he decided he was interested in me again. This time, I was the one who was ambivalent. This led to him taking a few buses to get to me during the summer to go to the beach with me, more than once. By that time, I didn't care one way or the other, but I was flattered by the attention. Both he and I were not of the economic class to have cars while we lived at college.

My mother was thrilled that someone would like me enough to go to that trouble, and she thought I should like him back. That probably made me care even less, and I probably was still angry that he had disappeared when I had liked him.

I tend to be curious about what my old boyfriends are doing now, and social media makes that easy. I did find him. While I knew him at Harvard, he was planning to become a doctor, but he didn't follow that path, going into finance instead. He told me he had gotten married late and had a baby when he was about fifty. What is it about these men I dated?

The Disappearing Dentist (1972)

"I will be right back."

And that was the end of that short fling. He never returned. I never saw him again.

His name was Dean Moretti, a dental student soon to graduate. There was something about him that was sleazy, and I didn't trust him. We had gone out just a couple of times. On this last date, we were in a fraternity house watching a movie. He told me he was looking in the obituaries for a dentist who passed away, so he could find a dental practice to buy. I remember being shocked and disgusted at the time, but I guess it is a common thing to do. Our conversation went downhill from there, and I guess we both decided this was not meant to be. So he got up and said he would be right back. And that was that. I thought to myself, *good riddance.* That brief relationship left a sour taste in my mouth. However, I am not afraid of dentists at all.

I had a lot of other short relationships in college, but nothing to write home about—or write here about!

Chapter 7

The Great Love (1973)

"Joe has a friend from school he thinks you will like,
and we want to set you up with him. He will be an usher at the wedding,
but hopefully you can meet him before that,"
Linda, my best college friend, told me.

After my unhappy freshman year with my unhappy freshman roommate, Linda, one of my college gang, and I roomed together for the next two years. Freshman year, Linda had roomed with Joanne of the "socks" comment fame. They had been friends in high school.

Finally, in senior year both Linda and I had single dorm rooms. She and I used to go out to meet men at mixers and frat parties and clubs. Senior year she was dating Joe, whom she met at a club. He wasn't a college student and was attending a nearby vocational school. We, her friends, didn't like him at all. We thought he was crude and didn't treat her very well. He also had a bad temper. Therefore, I wasn't really interested in meeting one of his friends.

Linda was getting married in a couple of months, in the middle of senior year. I was to be a bridesmaid, and the guy she wanted to fix me up with was to be an usher. This is what she told me about him: "His name is Alan. He's Jewish [neither Linda nor Joe was] and plays in a band. He has had this girlfriend for about five years, a grad student, but now he is with someone he met while she was working at Dunkin' Donuts near his school. He is just using her for sex though. He said he would like to meet you. Joe and Alan aren't really friends, but Joe did ask him to be an usher."

Well, if there weren't red flags in that description! However, I perked up a little because being Jewish myself, I always felt more comfortable with Jewish men, although I have never had much luck with them! And I always liked musicians. And since Joe and Alan weren't really friends, that could be a positive. But we never did manage to meet before the wedding.

I figured we would meet at the rehearsal dinner the night before the wedding. By then I was looking forward to meeting this mystery man, so I was a little disappointed that Alan wasn't there. His band had a gig that night. So, I added to my list of red flags that he was irresponsible and didn't even manage to show up at the rehearsal of a wedding he was in.

The first time I saw Alan was on the limo ride to the church. Although we had both brought dates to the wedding, they were not in the bridal party limo, nor were they seated with us at the reception. The bride nearly fainted from the heat in the limo, and it was Alan who took care of things—asked if she was okay, opened the windows, and then helped her out of the limo. He was too nice—and way too cute—not to like. I probably fell in love right then.

I had brought Jeff, that casual boyfriend of mine of three years, to the wedding as my date. Alan had also brought a date with him—Peggy, the girl from Dunkin' Donuts. She was seated at the table with my date, so I later heard all about what went on at that table. Now remember this was 1973, and they were likely sitting with some older relatives. She announced to the table that she and Alan had been "shacking up for a while," which apparently shocked some of the guests.

However, Alan and I didn't care what was going on at that table. We were having a perfectly fine time with each other at the head table. I was completely smitten.

At the end of the reception, Jeff, Alan, Peggy, and I spoke briefly. I didn't know until her name was said which of Alan's two "girlfriends" she was, the grad student or the donut girl. But I can remember everything about her to this day.

She was nothing much to look at. Average height. Average weight. Mousy brown hair, medium length, a little stringy. Really turned up nose. She was wearing a simple pinkish red dress that had a tie around the waist, which was hanging undone. And clunky shoes with chunky heels. I was sizing up what I thought was probably my competition. Turns out she was the donut girl; I probably had much more in common with his student girlfriend.

Alan took my phone number, and I was sure he would call. His parents lived in a suburb of Boston, so he wasn't far away. He was still at that school in Boston, having dropped out of college. And he told me he was living with his parents at the time. I never asked about the "shacking up" story. I didn't want to know.

I was home in Lynn at the time because it was that long January break that colleges had between semesters. My mother was in the hospital for a while at this time for mental issues that were a result of her physical issues, and I was alone with my father, which was pretty uncomfortable. I mentioned Alan to him in our limited conversations. He said, "I wouldn't hold my breath waiting for him to call if I were you." As I write this, I am wondering why my parents were always so negative.

I waited and waited for that phone call. Finally, about two weeks after we met, Alan called. It was now the end of January, and I was almost back at school. My single dorm room would be convenient for dating, I mused.

I was still "dating" Jeff, but he was away at school again, with the new habit of calling me at 10 p.m.—when he did call. I had pretty much lost all interest in him after I met Alan. Alan and I laughed about those 10 p.m. calls, and shortly thereafter I called it quits with Jeff. Although Alan was more available than Jeff ever was, he was available to me only on Tuesday nights and Saturday nights. It seemed at the time to be enough for the beginning of a relationship after hardly ever seeing Jeff at all. And Alan told me that he wasn't seeing anyone else at the time, neither the student nor Peggy. Those relationships were "over."

Alan would visit my dorm on Tuesday nights and then again on Saturdays. He would stay Saturday night and leave on Sunday. Alan was a big TV fan, and I had no television in my dorm room. He used to schlep his big color TV with him so he could watch *Star Trek*, his favorite show. Although I was there cuddling with him while he watched *Star Trek*— and I have been involved with more than one *Star Trek* fan in my life—I never actually "watched" even one episode of the show.

I was on cloud nine while I was dating Alan. The relationship lasted through February, March, and April of my senior year in college. I assumed he wasn't seeing anyone else, since he was available to see me every weekend and frequently called me. I took him at this word he was done with the other two women.

I was so proud to be dating him. I remember being so happy when he would call my dorm room that after I spoke to him, I would start cleaning the room, even if it was late at night. Now, that is happiness. I hate cleaning.

All the students who worked at the front desk of my dorm, where he would have to sign in, would say how cute and charming he was. Yes, men were allowed in the dorms when I was at college as long as they signed in.

After about three months, Alan suddenly disappeared. I had no idea what the problem was. Everything had been going fine. It was by now the very end of April, right before my college graduation at the beginning of May. I called him to ask where he had been. He said he needed to come over and talk. Uh-oh. You know what that means.

"You remind me of Barbara," he said. "and if I was going to be serious with anyone, it would be her, since we already went out for five years. But I am probably going to move out West to California or Arizona soon anyway."

This was all a complete lie. Maybe it was his intention at the time, but none of that happened. As far as I know, he never got back together with

Barbara, although they remained phone friends. And I am going to venture a guess that he never left Peggy and was probably living with her while he spent his Tuesday and Saturday nights with me.

About a week after this discussion, I graduated from college; my graduation was really sad for me because Alan had just dumped me. And I really had no idea why.

Meanwhile, my friend Linda did finish college and graduate with us, having married in the middle of senior year, and we kept in touch for a while. We have reconnected casually on social media, and I have meant to write to her for a long time. She and Joe did not stay married. We friends were not surprised.

Chapter 8

Return of the Great Love

"So we will start dating and then we will move in together.
Then, if all goes well, we will get married."
Alan and I were in a park near my house
at 3 a.m. on a cold November morning in 1973.

But let's go back to May when I graduated from college, still crushed from the blow of Alan dumping me. I lived through that summer after graduation, bruised as I was. In fact, I had quite a pleasant summer, much to my surprise.

I started looking for a job in public relations or corporate writing, without much luck. Having no job or other means of support, I went home to Lynn after graduation to live with my parents. And there, literally in my backyard, I met my summer crush.

Summer "Fling" (1973)

There was another house in back of ours—literally in our yard. The couple who lived there had one daughter, about five years older than I was. When I was in first grade, Paula used to walk me to school. The next year, she moved on to junior high, and we rarely saw each other. Now that she was well out of high school, she continued to live at home with her parents. She had no job and rarely went out of the house. I don't know quite what was going on with her, but I never pictured her dating. Well, apparently, she was dating someone.

One evening at the end of May, I had just come home from a shopping trip with my mother. As I got out of the car, I saw Paula and some guy walking up the stairs and into her house. A minute later, he came walking out. We started to talk and he asked me out. I asked him, "Are you dating Paula?" He said he had just seen her a couple of times, and she was kind of strange.

Jerry was very nice looking, a few years older than I. After talking with him a while, I said I would go out with him. I was desperate for a rebound relationship so I could forget about Alan, and I didn't need to go any farther than my yard for this one.

But while I was a straight-A student and now had a degree, Jerry wasn't very intellectual. Not that Alan was, but he was pretty smart. Jerry was just kind of fun; he filled a need when I was lonely at home after being in college and then being dumped by Alan. And I felt secure; I didn't have to worry about him not liking me or not being with me. I think we went out most evenings. It was just fun. We went out all summer and into the fall.

I did eventually get a job in late summer. Not a perfect job by any means, but a job. I was a medical biller in the basement of someone's house. The someone was my boss, and she was pretty mean. I worked there for about a year.

The Day That Will Live Forever (1973)

Back to the park at three in the morning. It was November 13. And the man saying those words, planning out our lives, was Alan.

November 12: the day that will live in infamy. The phone rang at my parents' house. My father answered and said it was for me. It must have been one of those few nights that I wasn't out with Jerry. It was Alan on the phone. I hadn't heard a word from him since that May night when he dumped me.

Overjoyed? Best night of my life? Yup. He wanted to come over and talk. Last time he wanted to come over and talk it was to break up with me. I knew it couldn't be that this time. I was beside myself with happiness. We walked to the Commons, a park a couple of blocks from my house. We sat there on a bench and talked all night, after which my father accused me of doing all kinds of things I didn't do since I had "stayed out all night." I told him I was talking in the park, and I was telling the truth—as I probably did most of the time, since I was a really good kid. I suppose he didn't believe me. And frankly I cannot imagine how we had so much to talk about that it took that many hours. All I remember about that conversation are the words that are at the beginning of this chapter, and my making sure that he was actually now available and wouldn't change his mind again. I would think "I still love you" or "I never got over you," must have been in there somewhere.

Alan had it all planned out. We were going to start going out, and then we would move in together, and then we would get married. For me it was a dream come true. I was never happier in my life!

And so it happened—well, most of it. We did start going out, and it was all wonderful. Remember the Playboy Clubs? He had a "key" to the clubs, so we often went to the one in Boston. Despite the waitresses with their cottontails, they had great music for dancing and great food. They also had good grasshoppers, which was my drink of choice: white crème de cacao, green crème de menthe, and cream. After eleven each night, they would start serving brunch. We danced, we drank, we ate, and I was in heaven.

Another heavenly memory took place on New Year's Eve of that year, about a month and a half after we started dating again. I accompanied him to his New Year's Eve gig. He played the keyboard. I was so proud to be with this cute guy. Doesn't every girl love a musician? I was even happy to help him carry that cumbersome, heavy keyboard around.

One more memory of those days: I came out of my basement medical billing job one day to find Alan sitting there waiting for me with a bouquet of flowers. He was that kind of guy—sometimes.

The Move-In (1974)

In February—it was now 1974—my parents wanted to move from the house I grew up in to something smaller. Since I wasn't home much at this point, they wanted to know if they should move someplace with a bedroom for me or not. I brought the subject up with Alan, asking him if I could just move in. At the time he was living outside of Boston in a two-bedroom apartment with another couple. So I joined the threesome, making us a foursome. (As I am now reading this again, proofreading it, it occurs to me—after all these decades—that he likely moved in when he was with someone. Why would a single guy move in with a couple? Of course! Read on, and you, too, will figure it out!)

Being the last one of the four to move in, I was intimidated, especially by the "other girlfriend." We didn't talk very much, but I always felt she had control of the kitchen since she was living there first. She was also kind of a snob. Or maybe I just felt inferior to her. In any case, I would rush home from work to get to the kitchen and make dinner for Alan and me before she got there. By this time Alan was done with technical school and repairing appliances.

I wasn't a very capable cook then, and I still don't really enjoy cooking. Alan taught me to make a dish with fish, rice, and stewed tomatoes in which you didn't have to cook anything beforehand. My kind of cooking: you just put the ingredients in a dish and bake it.

I baked it in a CorningWare® dish that I still have. Do you have any items that are really, really old—and if you told the people who gave them to you or used them with you, they would be really surprised you still had them? That is my dish that Alan bought for me. I still use it forty-five years later!

I remember very little about living in that apartment except it had white walls and was always very neat—and of course, I remember that Alan had a waterbed. It was one of the old waterbeds, where you would constantly have to get the air bubbles out.

One night when we were giving a party, I was helping Lisa, the other woman who lived there, roll meatballs from ground beef. I remember she remarked it was kind of gross, which was one of the few conversations we ever had. She was wearing an emerald green velvet pantsuit. Funny the things you remember. And she and her boyfriend, our roommates, did eventually get married.

The Big Chill (1974)

We were together (this time) for two Valentine's Days. I hadn't yet officially moved in the first Valentine's Day we were together. Nonetheless, the big chill began.

Being a very insecure 23-year-old, I was expecting flowers for Valentine's Day, that dreaded of holidays. Well, Alan got me a little wooden penguin who was holding flowers, knowing I had a real thing for penguins and collected them. I was so disappointed, but I couldn't tell him, so I sulked. Verbal communication wasn't—and still isn't—my strong point (fear of rejection). He asked me what was wrong, but I guess I didn't tell him for a while. So he threw the penguin at the wall. The event doesn't seem like a really big deal, but not too long after that things started to go downhill, and I can't trace it back to anything except that event.

Continuing the downhill slide, sometime after that Valentine's Day and after I moved in shortly thereafter, Alan started to lose interest in me. He even lost interest in himself, not washing his hair, etc. Finally, I got up the courage to ask what the problem was; he said he didn't know, but it was *his* problem. He finally did tell me something that hurt so much, it affects me to this day. He told me our pheromones were incompatible, except he was a lot blunter. He said it would either resolve itself or it wouldn't, and if it didn't, "We will be like the people in *The Way We Were*," a tearjerker of a movie that was popular at the time. So the power in the relationship was now all his, as I waited.

Looking back, I guess I would have saved myself a lot of misery if I had never gone back with him in the first place after he dumped me in college. But—I was young and in love.

We stayed together and eventually even moved to Florida that August. At some later time, I did ask him about the "issue," and he said it was resolved. But things never seemed the same again to me. I was more insecure than ever, and that led to all kinds of problems.

The Big Move (1974)

The summer after the "penguin" incident, before we moved to Florida, we spent a lot of time at the racetrack betting on greyhounds. I am not a gambler at all; in fact, because of my father's gambling habit, I don't gamble at all. I don't even buy lottery tickets. I don't like casinos. But I did get into the greyhounds that summer, especially one of the champions, who was named Stretch. To this day, I want to adopt a retired racing greyhound, but I keep getting little dogs instead.

The most I ever won at the races was about $67 on a perfecta. But Alan did okay that summer and saved everything he won. One day he saw an ad for a job repairing appliances in Florida and decided to apply. Since he had talked about moving to California or Arizona as one of the reasons he was dumping me the first time, I guess he was looking for a warmer climate. He got the job and asked me to move with him. Although I knew I would go in the end, I voiced some concern about moving with him.

I think I felt as if he would go with or without me, and I wanted to be with him. He claimed he really wanted me to move with him. He used the money he had won from the racetrack to hire a truck to move us all the way down the coast. We drove to Florida, taking a vacation along the way, and it was a great vacation. Things were very good. Obviously, I didn't think twice about leaving that medical billing job!

The Other Women

Besides the Valentine's Day incident, there was another issue. Remember those two girls? Barbara, with whom he had the five-year relationship and with whom he was going to get back together once upon a time? And Peggy, the one whom I met at the wedding, the girl from the doughnut shop? Well, neither one of them really left his life. Barbara had some mental issues, he claimed, which was the reason she would often call, him, even at 11 p.m. He would always talk to her. I was already so insecure in the relationship that it really annoyed me. I told him it bothered me, but he continued to talk to her when she called. And Peggy, whom he used for sex? He told me that she had given him an ultimatum, and since he didn't want to marry her, she went off and married someone else, moved to Missouri, and had a baby. But, he added, she "wasn't happy." And I don't think they ever stopped communicating with each other in secret.

Okay. I must confess. Back when we lived in the apartment before we moved to Florida, I had a good snoop through Alan's bureau drawers when he was at work. It was in the bottom drawer that I found evidence of those two women. I know. Lots of people, including me, keep mementos from old relationships, so it wasn't really a big deal. And if I didn't want to find anything, I shouldn't have looked. I found some letters and photos of Barbara, sunning herself at a New England beach she spent summers at. Since Alan was so cute, I thought she would probably be beautiful. She wasn't. And I remember finding a note or letter from Peggy saying that she still had the necklace he had given her—and something about being there for her when her mother was ill. And about how she would always love him. I never told him I had snooped!

The Big Breakup (1975)

Well, we had dated. And now we were living together. So the next of his promises was that we would get married. All these decades later, I still don't know exactly what happened. But here are some guesses, as I am now older and wiser—a little bit, anyway.

I was always very insecure in relationships. Perhaps it was my nature. Maybe that is why the things that my parents said to me really stuck. But that insecurity has never helped me in my relationships. And just maybe I have the tendency to choose men who keep me off balance instead of making me feel more secure.

When Alan and I were still in Massachusetts, we danced at the Playboy club. In Florida, we went fishing in this old boat he bought whose motor would often die in the middle of wherever we were. Our interests were getting farther apart, and we were not as compatible as we had been.

I was still very raw from his comments—as well as comments that I should lose weight, so I would look as I looked the day he met me at the wedding. I was all of five or six pounds heavier at this point. Maybe a size 12. And I still felt deep inside that things never went back sexually to where they were before his "episode" of whatever was going on with him.

I started to miss "home." I wanted my friends and family around when I got engaged. I wanted a bridal shower. I didn't have any close friends in Florida—just people I worked with. I complained about wanting to go home.

Everything combined to make a real mess. Alan said he had a ring, but he wouldn't give it to me until I "behaved." He told me I was a "borderline personality" and should go to see a therapist. So I did. The therapist told me that Alan (whom he did meet) was the one with the problems. Therapy didn't seem to help. I was just very angry at Alan. Some of it was my doing, and some of it was his.

As the summer went on in Florida, things went from bad to worse. Alan began nagging me about when I was going to move out. I was very dependent on him at the time, and I couldn't imagine staying down there, away from family and friends, without him. I did have a job I loved, but I don't know if I could have afforded to live by myself. I was working as an editor at the local daily newspaper, one of my favorite jobs to this day.

Shortly before we finally broke up, Alan said maybe he should go away for a few days. He went away for three days, saying he missed me when he got back. He never told me where he went—and I guess I was afraid to ask—but it was clear that he had gone to Missouri, or wherever Peggy was at the time. He had already told me that she wasn't happy with her husband and was leaving him.

I left Florida in August, never even seeing that ring—if there really was one—just one year after we had moved there. Masochistically on my part, I had Alan drive me all the way home in my car, after which he flew back. He dropped me at a college friend's house, where I stayed for a while, since I was too embarrassed to tell my parents what had happened. They never really liked or trusted Alan very much.

I had some work friends at the Florida newspaper that I kept in touch with right after I left. We lived and worked in a smallish town at the time, and Alan worked downtown near the newspaper offices. My friends reported to me that they saw a woman outside Alan's place of work just a few days after I left. Their description confirmed it was Peggy. Hmmm. I wasn't surprised. It sure didn't take long for him to bounce back to her, did it?

I had made Alan a beautiful scrapbook, which I ripped up in front of him during one of our dark times. Believe me when I say it didn't help matters, and that action was the definite beginning of the end. A few months after my return to Massachusetts, I recreated the scrapbook and sent it to him with a letter. I got a letter back from Peggy. She told me they were married and they were happy, and that I should now go on and get my own life because, "Alan's and my love has outlived your relationship and Barbara's." The kicker here is that I must have said something about November 12 in my letter to him—the day he called me and professed his love and said that we would eventually get married. She said that she, too, remembered that date because that is the day when she gave Alan the ultimatum. Wow. Talk about jumping from branch to branch.

Peggy had written the letter, but she made Alan sign it. He also wrote she was "a little" pregnant and to be "true to his marriage" he would be sending the scrapbook back. I never received it.

I blamed myself 100 percent for the demise of this relationship. That is why I still could not get over it decades later. I blamed myself because of my anger and my inability to communicate. In my mind, I knew that it is usually both people's doing, and some people are just not meant to be together. But I often think my shortcomings must be worse than anyone else's. I see women with addictions, abusive childhoods, and damaged psyches in relationships—possibly good relationships—and I wonder, "Why not me?"

Chapter 9

Mending a Broken Heart

"Oh, those Jews, they own all of the jewelry stores.
And when they shop for anything, they try to jew you down."

I got back to Boston from Florida in September of 1975. I got married in October of 1985. Those ten years were pretty dark dating years for me.

The Anti-Semites (1976)

Bob was a fix-up. I was introduced to him by some guy friends I shared a house with. He was French Canadian, not that that has anything to do with anything. He was not my physical type, but since he was a friend of a friend whom I trusted, I said I would meet him. He seemed nice enough. We went out several times. And I sure do remember the last date we had. We went out for Chinese food with his mother and two aunts. I don't know what started this conversation, but they began talking about how Jews own all the jewelry stores, and they used the anti-Semitic phrase "jewing someone down." Of course, they didn't realize I was Jewish, and I didn't tell them. And I never saw Bob again. I think that was the only time I personally ran into such blatant anti-Semitism.

The Mistake (1977)

Before the days of online dating, there were dating services. Being shy and never considering myself very popular, I joined one of these services, called Together, and began what I refer to as my "string of six-week relationships." My standards were not very high at the time, and most of the men they matched me up with were okay. I liked them and they liked me—for about six weeks, after which things got too serious for them.

Danny B. had curly dark hair and glasses and was on the short side—in other words, my type. I always suspected I liked shorter men because my father was tall and skinny. Danny was an optician at a well-known retail store. We were together for the usual six weeks or so, mostly every night, most of the time spent in my little room in the house I rented with four MIT graduates. A couple of things stand out about Danny. He was about 30, but his father was 80. And I learned a lesson from being with him. Birth control doesn't work if you don't use it. Enough said about that one.

The Disappearance (1978)

It was the seventies and I loved—and still love—to dance. Boston was full of discos at the time, so I would go, usually alone, to try to meet someone. The Copley Plaza Hotel in Boston had a disco party every weekend. That is where I met Dave Amsel.

Dave was short and chubby with thinning blond hair, not generally my "type," which was lots of dark hair including facial hair. He worked at his father's business selling candy bars and tobacco products to stores, so he always knew about the latest in candy bars. Back then, there was no internet, so it was more difficult to do any research on someone you were dating. I must have been unusually suspicious about this guy because the first thing I did was look him up in the phone book. I already knew what street he lived on in Boston, so I am not sure what I hoped to find in the phone book. Perhaps I wanted to see if I could find a woman's name. I was suspicious that he might be married. And I did find a woman's name. The phone book entry was printed as "Amsel, Lisa and David." It was odd, because he had given me his home phone number. So I called him a couple of times, and a woman answered the phone. I hung up. When I asked him about the woman who answered the phone, he told me it was "the cleaning lady." In the evening? In the phone book? Ya think? He denied being married. Of course.

I have no idea why I continued to see this man. Maybe I didn't want to believe he was married. I didn't even like him that much. And he wasn't very nice. We went away for a weekend to Saratoga, New York, to the famous horse races Saratoga Springs is known for. Between the business he helped to run and the horseracing, he seemed pretty shady.

During that weekend in Saratoga, Dave thought it appropriate to wear a canary yellow jumpsuit. Although jumpsuits were popular for women at that time, I don't think too many men would wear a yellow jumpsuit. When I told my friends about it, they said he must have looked like a canary. Well, I can tell you it wasn't terribly flattering, and he had a lot of chutzpah to wear it.

When I was dating Dave, I was living in my high-rise studio apartment with the gold shag carpeting in Framingham, Massachusetts. I loved that apartment. It was the first time I had ever lived alone except for my single dorm room my senior year in college.

The last time I saw Dave was at my apartment. I didn't even like him by this time; I was annoyed that I didn't know what was going on with him at home. Of course, I shouldn't have been seeing someone like that at all. Low self-esteem, I guess.

At some point during the evening, he was talking about a new candy bar they were selling. He went down to his car to get the candy to show it to me. He never came back.

That was the last I saw of Dave, but not the last I heard from him. At the time, I was taking tap dance lessons not far from where he lived in Brookline, a suburb of Boston. More than once I would come to my car after an evening class and find a little anonymous love note on my windshield. I knew the notes were from him. He called me several times after that. However, I was uninterested in ever seeing him again.

Chapter 10

A Change of Race

"Why do you have so much toilet paper?"
I asked Frankie when he opened his closet
to reveal a stack of toilet paper four feet high.

"Oh, I just like to keep stocked up."

Well-Stocked Frankie (1980)

Back in the seventies people noticed more than they do now if you were with someone of a different race. Now it is no big deal. I generally liked to date Jewish men, although I also dated men who weren't Jewish. And I did go through a phase of being attracted to African-American men. There were three.

I met Frankie at my apartment complex, the studio apartment with the gold shag carpeting. The complex was large enough to have its own little variety store, and that is where I met him. Sometimes he worked there, but he was also a security guard for the complex and had a law-enforcement type uniform. He also lived in my building. At first I thought he might be a police officer, but he wasn't. I am not generally into men with uniforms, so the uniform wasn't it. He just seemed really nice. I don't know whether or not my attraction to black men was in response to my father's racism.

Frankie was short and stocky. We were never really a couple. It was more of a friendship. And once when I was in his apartment—probably the only time—he opened a closet and in it were 50 or more rolls of toilet paper. That made an impression on me. I had never seen anyone, especially a single guy, stock up on paper goods before, including my own mother. But now I do that, although not quite to that extent. He would have done great during a pandemic!

Talking Ragtime (1983)

Then there was Curtis. I met him at a club in Boston. He was tallish, slim, and pretty cute. He even had a dimple or two. We dated for a while; actually, he was the last man I dated before I met my ex-husband in 1983. I had moved from my studio apartment to another nearby complex (where I later met my ex-husband). I had moved up to a first-floor one-bedroom where I could watch ducks walk around my patio. I loved that apartment.

Curtis was nice enough, but he talked "ragtime." What is that, you ask? Well, my father had this phrase, "talking ragtime," that really did apply to Curtis. Talking ragtime is talking and talking and not really making any sense at all. After some research, I found that it is usually applied to women in a misogynistic way, who "talk crazy at a certain time of the month."

That aside, Curtis would talk and talk, and I couldn't figure out what the point was; he went around and around in circles.

I was still "going out" with Curtis when I met my husband, although our relationship had run its course, and we were pretty much just friends at this point. I met Doug (my ex) at my apartment complex, where he also lived, in the early summer of 1983.

Fast forward to the Fourth of July. Curtis and I already had plans to go to the Charles River in Boston where seemingly millions of people gather every year for the Fourth of July concert with the Boston Pops, followed by fireworks. I was sitting there on the blanket with Curtis, and who should walk by? Doug, whom I had already started to date casually. He was with a woman as well, who, I later found out, was just a friend.

I remember telling Curtis right after Doug walked by, "I am going to marry that man." And I did just that.

Me Too

Then, there was Cookie, or Dr. Cook. But Cookie, although he is African American as well, really belongs in the next chapter.

Chapter 11

Me Too

"Well, I have no time to listen to your problems tonight.
Let me tell you about mine."
We were sitting in a Chinese restaurant when
Dr. Hartwell said these words to me.

Dr. Hartwell (1979)

When the Me Too Movement began and everyone began posting "Me Too," on social media, I honestly could not think of any time I had been sexually abused or assaulted in any way. Finally, a lightbulb went off. I thought of Patrick Hartwell, my therapist in the late seventies . . .

I had been to a therapist or two before, the first one being in Florida, when Alan told me I should see a therapist. This time it was to talk about my unsuccessful love life, which always, of course, led back to one parent or another. I found Dr. Hartwell in the phone book (remember those?); he was a Ph.D. psychologist and a hypnotherapist.

Dr. Hartwell was not particularly nice looking, but he was charming. He had been a Jesuit Brother before getting married, having two daughters, and then getting divorced. The therapy sessions soon turned into "massage sessions." It wasn't after too many sessions that vulnerable, needy, gullible me "fell in love" with my therapist—and I thought, he with me. Our sessions turned into dates. Most of the time they were in his office, since he really didn't want to be seen in public with a patient.

We did go out a couple of times, once to a Chinese restaurant and once to the ballet. These "dates" were scheduled as therapy sessions, and I believe he was charging my insurance company for these "sessions."

It didn't appear that Dr. Hartwell was accustomed to going out or dressing up. He had to dress up for the ballet, and he had on his fancy shoes. He broke a shoelace and had to tie his shoe with the short piece that was left. Funny the things you remember so many years later.

At the time I considered myself a consenting partner in this "relationship," but of course I wasn't. He was clearly abusing his power as a therapist.

He seemed to have some female friends who took really good care of him. He would often show me these meals that were all nicely covered in foil that one of this "friends"—a former nun—would prepare for him. He also complained that his ex-wife would not let him have unsupervised visits with his daughters, preteens at the time. He didn't give me a good answer when I asked him why, and I don't know why I didn't run for the hills.

After several months, he told me that he probably shouldn't be my therapist anymore. Eventually, I needed a therapist because of this experience.

Months later I read some shocking news in my local newspaper, *The Boston Herald*: Dr. Patrick Hartwell was being sued by a dozen women—all patients—for sexual abuse. I contacted the attorney who was mentioned in the article and told her my story. I joined the lawsuit, and we won. His license was taken away, and he moved to New Jersey to practice hypnotherapy. I never knew if he went to prison, but I did now know why his ex-wife would not allow him unsupervised visits with his daughters.

Cookie (1982)

A year or two after my episode with Dr. Hartwell, I began working as a technical writer at Wang Laboratories, a computer company north of

Boston. When I began the job, I was living in the studio with the gold shag carpeting, and then I moved to the one-bedroom with the ducks on my deck. Both places were 40 miles away from my job—but somehow I was drawn to the town I was living in.

It was 1982. My love life had not improved, and I was once again looking for a therapist for my trouble with men and my low-grade depression.

A friend at work was seeing a nearby therapist, and she recommended I go there, where there were several therapists. I didn't know any of them, and I wound up with Dr. Cook, a Harvard-educated psychiatrist. He was African American and very nice-looking. I nicknamed him Cookie. He was also flirtatious, which is exactly what I didn't need from a therapist, since I had told him about my issues with Dr. Hartwell.

I always looked forward to those days when I was going to see Cookie during my lunch break from work. I always tried to look my best and had a favorite outfit that I would wear some of those days. The outfit consisted of dark green harem pants, the pants that had elastic on the ankles and were popular at the time. The pants had an elastic waist, even though in those days an elastic waist was the style of the pants and not a necessity! I had a print blouse that I wore with those pants—and gold strappy sandals, which I thought went well with the rest of the outfit. Gold strappy sandals that I wore even if it was snowy!

Cookie and I didn't have dates or anything like that, but I developed a huge crush on him, which I felt he definitely initiated and promoted. We got into the habit of hugging after each session. I don't know who started that, but I cannot imagine that it was me, as I was pretty shy. Okay, maybe I wasn't so shy about certain things.

One day soon after I started seeing him, he told me he had just moved into a new house with a hot tub on the deck. He said he had daydreamed about me being with him in the hot tub. Well, of course, this got my attention, and I assumed he had an interest in me. Of course, this was completely inappropriate. At that point I didn't think I had done or said anything flirtatious at all. After a while of what didn't really seem like therapy to me, I asked him why we didn't just date, since we seemed very compatible. And he was single.

Of course he said we couldn't date, since I was his patient. I guess I was really looking more for a boyfriend than a therapist at this point. I said, "Well then, I will stop being your patient." Ultimately, we decided it was best that I wasn't his patient any longer.

He never apologized for anything. He said that everything he did was part of treatment, and that it was "transference." I transferred my feelings for an appropriate man onto him—and his responding to me was just part of the treatment. Bullshit. Double bullshit since I had already had a negative experience with a therapist that he knew about. I recently heard from another friend who worked with us that Cookie is still in practice all these years later in the very same place.

Chapter 12

Men at Work

"I got divorced and moved to an apartment where I couldn't have pets.
I loved my dog and couldn't have her with me,
so I shot her," explained Bryan.
Bryan was one of the men I dated whom I met at work.

Many people say it is a bad idea to date people you work with. Some companies even have policies against it because couples of different "levels" might get together, resulting in what might be an abuse of power or harassment. Someone might get promoted to be the other's boss, and then what? However, many people do meet at work. And yes, it can be quite difficult to work with someone after you have broken up. Been there, done that.

Bryan, the Dapper Dresser (1979)

The first time I ever dated someone from work was in 1979 at Prime, the first computer company I worked for. I had now been back from Florida for about four years. I had been doing temporary work and hadn't really had a job until I got this one. And I was at Prime for only six months before I got the technical writing job at Wang and switched companies.

I was hired as a secretary in the Marketing Department at Prime, although I had a college degree and wanted to do something with writing. The reason I left after six months was that they were hiring an editor in the department, and I wanted that position. The department manager pictured the editor as a "man," a nerd who just wanted to sit and edit all day. To me this seemed rather sexist, even in 1979, and I complained to him. I think I even threatened to sue him. Fortunately, I soon got the technical writing job at Wang.

During the six months I was at Prime, I had an "interesting" relationship. I was working for a couple of different people, but they were both in the same department, producing technical and marketing materials. There were three of us young women in the department, all around the same age, late twenties. One of the women, Diana, was a public relations professional who actually had a salary. The other two of us were more clerical and had an hourly wage. Cyndy was the other woman. She was really pretty, very petite, and had two children, who were already teenagers; she had had her first child at 15. This was a real shocker to me at the time! She was not married at this time, but she once had been.

The three of us were friendly at work. Diana started telling us about a man she had recently started dating. She never gave us his name but told us about how his closet was so organized that all his shirts were lined up by color. She thought it was unusual he should be so fussy about his clothes—and have so many of them.

We all worked with a guy named Bryan Wallace. He was on the short and stocky side with red, thinning hair and a red face to match, full of acne scars. Despite the fact he wasn't very good looking, he was always very well dressed, with colorful shirts and bow ties. He was also very friendly and helpful, and everyone liked him.

Since I was at this job for only six months, everything happened in a short time frame. At some point, I started working primarily for Bryan, and I remember developing a crush on him. The whole department often went out for a long lunch on Fridays. One Friday we were at lunch, and Bryan had a "little" too much to drink. I was in charge of his schedule at the time, and I knew he had a meeting that afternoon. I left lunch before he did and went back to work. He never came back to work that day. I called him at home. There were no cell phones back then. Someone had given me his number, but I still felt pretty weird calling him. I told him he had a meeting, and he said he wasn't coming back to work. Don't ask me why he appealed to me at all, especially after that.

Shortly after this episode, Diana confessed to Cyndy and me that Bryan was the person she had been dating. It all made sense: the closet with all the fashionable clothes. When she finally told us, they had already stopped seeing each other, so I told her that I was interested in him. She said I was free to date him because they were done, and she gave me her blessing. I needed it!

Why did I find it oh-so appealing that Bryan was a drinker (red face and all) and couldn't come back to work after lunch because he was so drunk?

We started dating. Diana was the past, except for him telling me some pretty personal stuff about her. I was the new girl. He was nice, and I don't remember him getting drunk on any dates. Although we kept our relationship quiet at work, both Diana and Cyndy knew about it.

I was at his apartment around the time of his thirty-sixth birthday. He told me how half his life was over, but he was going to turn things around for the second half of his life. I imagine that meant stopping drinking. That is when he told me about his dog. He'd had a dog when he was married (he had no children), and when he got divorced, he got the dog. But then he moved to a place where he couldn't have a dog. Did he give the dog to a friend? No. Did he take the dog to a shelter? No. Did he put an ad in the paper, looking for someone to take the dog? No. He couldn't have the dog, so he shot the dog. I kid you not.

Was I disgusted enough to break up with him at this point? Nope. I tried to be "understanding" and supportive. But then, after three months of dating him, he started disappearing, becoming more distant. Diana said she saw his car at Cyndy's house. Yup. He had moved on to the third young woman in the department. Diana was history. I was history. Cyndy was now "it." I don't think he and Cyndy lasted long either. But by then I had left the company.

I didn't leave Prime until I had a new job. This was a "real job," salaried, as a technical writer for software applications at Wang. I remember how happy I was to start at twelve thousand dollars a year! And as a bonus, I found a few men at this job as well. I started this job at the end of 1979 and stayed until February of 1986, when I left to raise a family, and frankly because I was tired of it. I had gotten married in October of 1985.

The Married Man (1980)

Mark Dorman and I started working at the company at around the same time. He was also a technical writer and was assigned to the same project as I was. There were four of us on the project, which consisted of writing about thirty books for a software application, and I soon became the project leader. Mark was a quiet man, and at first I paid no real attention to him. He was older than I by eight years. He was married and had two small children whose pictures he had pinned to his office bulletin board. They were adorable, especially his six-year-old daughter.

Mark was Jewish; he was also a chain smoker, probably the only smoker I ever dated. He was around five feet nine, with salt and pepper hair, of average weight, and kind of cute. We became friends after a short while, and the friendship evolved into something more.

Yes, I knew he was married. And I had not ever knowingly gone out with a married man—except the candy salesman, but he never admitted to being married, and I had no real proof.

Of course, Mark was "unhappily married." As we became closer, he told me that his wife, Wendy, had cheated on him, not once but twice. He didn't trust her anymore and thought about leaving. Our relationship became very romantic, probably because it was illicit. We kissed on the elevator between floors and had long conversations in each other's offices.

At the time we became friends, I was living in a house in a Boston suburb with four MIT graduates, who were all male. It was totally platonic; they were friends of friends. I lived there in my little third-floor room for three years, after which I moved to the studio apartment with the gold shag carpet. It is Mark who moved me into that apartment. He had a truck, and he took my few items of furniture and drove the forty miles to my new apartment. That was when our actual affair began.

One day, shortly after my move, he came over to my apartment and told me he had left his wife. He was rattled, but also happy that we could be together. He took a bath in my new apartment to calm himself down. The next day he went back to his wife.

When they say not to date someone you work with because it is hell if you break up, believe them. I become more attached to people than some women do, I admit. I was crushed when he returned to his wife, but I was also angry. And we worked so closely together, I couldn't get away from him. By now, everyone in the department knew what was going on and could probably hear our angry discussions in his office. Most of the anger was probably coming from me, because Mark was more of a passive type. This uncomfortable situation lasted for quite a while.

Mark did eventually leave the company a while before I did. He moved halfway across the country to take a similar job at another company. Those were the days when everyone was looking for technical writers, and companies were even willing to move people to their new jobs and new states. When Mark moved, his wife did not go with him. He did leave her. But by then, our relationship was too damaged to repair.

A year or two after Mark left the company, my boss told me she had spoken to him on the phone. By this time, I was engaged, so my boss gave Mark the news. She told me he said congratulations. She thought he might want to talk to me himself, but he said he was happy for me and thought it best if we didn't talk to each other. That was the last I heard about Mark Dorman. I still think of him, and when I do, I think of him fondly. He was one of my favorite men.

Bolero (1982)

Back in the eighties, when I was at Wang, those touchy, feely team-building classes were popular. I was a supervisor for a couple of years, so I attended several of those workshops. Bob Lacroix taught most of them. I was interested in the work that he did and thought it would be fun to have his job. He told me about the degree he got to do this work, which was a master's degree at Harvard. And I did apply to the program while I was at Wang. I finished three of the eight classes. No, I didn't get thrown out of the Harvard Graduate School of Education. Harvard didn't design its programs to be taken part time or by people with regular jobs. The classes were in the afternoons. They did allow a few people to go part time, and I was one of the few allowed to do that. However, I had to leave work hours early to get to the classes. After a while I just got tired of it, since I worked about forty miles from Harvard, and I lived about forty miles from both work and Harvard.

My relationship with Bob Lacroix wasn't much more successful than my stint at Harvard. We became friends. As one of those women constantly seeking the approval from men that I didn't get from my father, I remember being happy that he had chosen me above all the other people in his classes to be friendly with. But I knew he was married; he wore a wedding band. After we had been friends for a couple of years, his wife left him to "find herself." He told me she started wearing "army boots," so I guess that was his way of explaining why she left.

One night I invited him over for dinner. This was in 1982. I was living in the one-bedroom apartment with the ducks on the deck, where I shortly thereafter met my future husband.

I was very hopeful and excited about this dinner. I pictured a very romantic evening. I figured that one of the most romantic pieces of music must be "Bolero," which was used in the 1979 movie *10* with Bo Derek. So I got the record (yes, vinyl) from the library.

And it just didn't happen. I don't know why it didn't, but it didn't. On either side. Once he was at my apartment, there just wasn't much romantic interest on either side. I don't know if "Bolero" even ever got played. I was disappointed and a little surprised, as I think he was. So we remained friendly at work, but eventually drifted apart as even friends.

One of My Favorite Friends (1982)

Peter Mendoza came to work as a technical writer a couple of years after I started working at Wang. By this time, I was no longer a technical writer; I had switched to copyediting because I wasn't interested in becoming more technical; I had gone back to my journalistic roots.

I was assigned to be Peter's editor for a technical manual he wrote. He was a pretty technical guy and wrote more technically oriented manuals than I ever did. He would frequently stop by my office to chat, and told me years later (yes, I did see him again years later) that it was because he "liked" me. Problem was he was married. He was very cute. Tall and thin, even though that wasn't usually my type. He had lots of curly dark hair and glasses. He also looked a little exotic (turns out he later found out that he is a quarter Filipino.)

We started going out to lunch together, just the two of us—quite often. I so wished he weren't married. But nothing ever happened. No kisses. No hand holding. Nothing.

Decades later he told me that things had almost happened. I don't remember being aware of it. I often have no clue when men are interested in me. Peter told me about specific incidences when we were together, and what I wore. I remember no details at all about those lunches. He also told me that one day he nearly came to visit me at my studio apartment.

I don't know if there was any talk in the department about us. I guess there likely was. But mostly we had different circles of work friends. He had some guy writer friends who were pretty technical. I had mostly editor girlfriends. Peter didn't stay in the department too long. He transferred to a department where he could actually write software instead of just writing about it. Not too long after that, he left the company entirely. Once he left the department, I don't think we went out for lunch anymore. Maybe that is why he left the department.

But, as I have already said, that wasn't the last I ever saw of Peter. But you will have to read on. He was cute and he was smart and he was nice and he was funny. One of my very favorite men I have known.

Chapter 13

The Married Years (1985–2001)

I met my ex-husband in June of 1984. We lived in the same apartment complex and met at the pool. Not too long after that we moved in together at a different complex. We got engaged on Valentine's Day in 1985 and were married the following October. I was 34 years old when I got married.

In 1993 we relocated from Massachusetts to California, so anything that happened after 1993 happened in California.

The marriage ended in 2001. This book is not about my marriage, and thus this is a very short chapter. My ex-husband was fine. He had no bad habits; nothing like infidelity or addiction or abuse or anything like that ended things. He is the father of our two wonderful children (adults now), and that is all I have to say about that. This is a dating memoir.

Chapter 14
The Rebirth (The Epiphany)

"I might consider putting you in my dance troupe if you lose some weight,"
my jazz instructor told me. I was completely crushed.
I cried while driving home that night and quit jazz classes right then.
The cellist-turned-exotic-dancer made it into the group.
The not-too-bright blonde with the pet raccoons
she brought to class on a leash made it into the group.
But I was not thin enough. I wasn't fat. I just wasn't "thin enough."

I tend to have passions in my life that change every several years. Some people are passionate about the same thing for their entire lives. I sometimes envy them; they seem to have such direction. I am on my third passion now.

My first was dancing. I danced as a child. And then when I returned from Florida, in my mid-twenties, I started taking jazz dance in Boston with a vehemence, three or four times a week, often more than one class a day. As with most things in my life, it became about a man. I became infatuated with my gay jazz teacher. I made it to the front of the class, but I was never good enough. I was never thin enough. It all ended in tears a couple of years after I started when Mr. Instructor didn't put me in the dance troupe he had just formed because I needed to lose some weight. I was destroyed, and that was the end of my jazz dancing—and my dreams of Broadway. I did move on to become a great tap dancer and tap instructor. I did a little performing too. And that never involved a man. Oh, wait—maybe eventually it did.

I always loved music and had taken classical piano lessons in junior high and high school for six years. I was okay at it. Enter the music passion decades later.

Near the end of my marriage, I decided I wanted to take piano lessons again. I wanted to learn jazz piano. I went to a local music store to see if they could recommend any teachers. I knew I wanted a male teacher. Something was going on in my mind about my marriage. I had always loved men who played an instrument, particularly piano—like my great love, Alan.

The music store recommended a couple of instructors. I called and left messages with them. One of them called me back and sounded perfect. He could teach me how to play jazz. I guess you can predict what happened next. No, not quite.

The Piano Teacher (2000)

Terry taught from the basement of his home. He was cute. He had salt and pepper curly hair and was not too tall. His hands always smelled like toast and jam, as he had two little girls, and my lessons were after breakfast. But in addition to being cute, he was an artist, a pianist, a creative soul. I had done all sorts of artistic endeavors my entire life—dancing, piano, a little acting, a little drawing, songwriting, poetry, writing. And I had married an engineer. They say opposites attract. Maybe. I had forgotten there were men who shared my interests, and at this point in my life, I was longing for that.

I could say Terry and I flirted, but it was probably just my imagination. Ah! There goes my insecurity and lack of confidence. I often think no one decent would flirt with me. So let's keep it that we both flirted. I took it a step further with obsessive infatuation. He inspired me in so many ways.

My piano lessons and Terry began a rebirth for me. I had wanted a master's degree ever since I graduated college, but I already had loans and figured I couldn't afford it. Now I wanted to get a master's degree in music. I didn't have the background to get accepted into a music program, but

I did get accepted into a master's program in humanities where I could focus on music history, so I did that. It took me seven years to get the degree, but I did it.

My rebirth included a trip to Paris—I had never been to Europe—although I was still married and my whole family went together. Terry had recently taken his wife to Paris, so I needed to go to Paris as well; he advised me about the museums I should see. And although I was always a reader, I started hanging around in bookstores and seemed to be attracting artistic types, including a clerk at a Barnes and Noble who told me, without even knowing me at all, that I must read Salman Rushdie's *The Ground Beneath Her Feet,* a love story about a singer. I never did finish it. Decades younger than I, he talked to me every time I went into the store.

My life seemed to be coming together in mysterious ways. Everyone I met was connected to someone else, and it was all connected to music. I even made a drawing of this, calling it the Circle of Epiphany. I finally got rid of it, but really wish I still had it.

I didn't really get too far in learning how to play jazz piano, which is incredibly difficult, especially if you are used to playing classical. And when Terry told me his wife was pregnant, I couldn't deal with it, and I stopped taking lessons. I guess I had imagined their marriage was on the rocks. Immediately, I threw myself into the office of a therapist.

What was I thinking anyway? Nothing ever happened between us at all, but I think I needed my fantasies. I haven't seen Terry in a really long time, but I think of him fondly. He was the impetus that pushed me from my marriage. Whether or not that was a good thing, I really don't know. I used to have occasional regrets about breaking up my family, but not so much any longer. My life would have been so different if I had stayed. But I think things ultimately turned out better for us all . . . I hope.

Stopping my piano lessons was not the end of my music passion. I continued with my master's degree classes, I continued to tap dance, and I signed up for a music-and-computers class at the local junior college in the fall of 2001. That is where I met Adam.

Chapter 15

The Rebound

Someone stared at us and Adam said,
"I think they are probably looking at me because I am so handsome."
And he was serious. Adam and I were strolling around in Macy's,
he with his suspenders and beret.

In the winter of 2001, after my marriage ended, but before I physically left the house, I decided to take a music class at the local junior college. I was still in my music-passion phase and thought maybe I could get back to my love of songwriting. The class was music and technology. There I met Adam.

A Flower on the Keyboard (2001)

Adam was about my age, whereas the rest of the class was quite a bit younger. It wasn't a very large class, maybe fifteen people. I noticed him because he was the only man of my age in the class, and he was kind of cute in an overweight, teddy bear kind of way. Our first conversation occurred at one of our first weekly classes when he asked if I had any hand lotion. I did happen to have some in my purse; it was this purple flowery smelling stuff, but he took some anyway. We became friendly in class, and then I started finding little gifts on my keyboard when I came to class every week, maybe a flower or some other small token.

It was a night class, and Adam and I started going out for a bite to eat after class and having long talks in the school or restaurant parking lot.

I was still living with my husband at the time, and I still feel bad about doing this. However, the relationship served as an impetus for me to finally figure out exactly how to end my marriage and move out of the house. I knew I wanted to go, I had told my husband a few months before this that I was leaving, and I had moved to the sofa.

In May, around the time the class was ending, Adam told me he loved me. As he had promised, he wrote a song for me as the final assignment. He also wrote me many poems, since he was a pianist, a poet, and a songwriter.

The Summer Move

I moved into my own home in June. During that summer, Adam and I saw each other every weekend. Our first big outing after I moved was a weekend away in Monterey. We were both looking forward to this weekend. He couldn't wait to show me some of the places he knew in Monterey, since he had grown up there.

The weekend was kind of a bust. Adam was hours late picking me up to even start the getaway, and I was already annoyed. And we had such high expectations of this weekend together that almost anything would have been a letdown.

The Fair

A couple of months later, near the end of the summer, was the county fair. Months before, when we were still in music class together, Adam had told me that he always enters his poems in the fair, as did his much younger friend who was also in the class. He added that his poems always won ribbons. He knew I had written poetry, and he urged me to enter my poems too. The problem was I hadn't written a poem in decades. So I wrote one. Just one. And I entered it into the fair. And I heard no more and thought no more about it.

We went to the fair together, along with my daughter, his poet friend from class, and a close friend of mine who was visiting from out of state.

When we walked into the main exhibit hall, my daughter called me over and said, "Look over there." Over there was my poem with a blue ribbon and a sign that said, "Best of Show." I was shocked.

My friend and my daughter could not believe the look on Adam's face when he saw that I had won Best of Show—and, incidentally, neither he nor his friend had won anything. My daughter, who had entered a poem in the young people's poetry competition (she was about 13) won a first-place prize.

The look on Adam's face was not a happy one. Adam wasn't happy for me, but instead he was upset that I had won and he hadn't. After all, I had never entered before and he had entered every year and had apparently won ribbons every year. He told me that the judges for the contests were "just some ladies from the garden club." I should have ended this relationship right then.

The Fade Out

Adam was definitely a transition man. He was kind of cute and charming, but he wasn't very nice to me. We had some good times, mostly at the beginning; we used to go out to eat—this was when the class was still going on—and get a couple of dishes and mix them together. I am not quite sure what the point of this was, but it was our "thing."

Almost as soon as it began as a real relationship—because I was now living on my own—things began to sour. Adam became uninterested in a physical relationship and then said he didn't want a relationship at all. I pushed, and I don't know why I bothered. Adam was not ambitious or educated, did not take care of himself physically, and he was insulting to me. More than once he said to me, "Well, after all, you don't have the body of an eighteen-year-old." I looked pretty good for forty-nine.

And I had my own home. Granted, it wasn't a new house. It wasn't updated with the newest kitchen and bathroom fixtures, but it was nice enough. It was a two-story house in a decent neighborhood with three bedrooms, two baths, and a garage and yard. My two kids lived with me most of the time. Adam, on the other hand, lived in what I called a "hovel." It was a little apartment attached to the back of a home, not even deserving of its own street number, but just one of those half numbers, like 365½. I would not be criticizing where he lived if he hadn't continually made fun of my house and all the "white plastic things in the kitchen." I had white cabinets and not enough of them, so I had a self-standing white unit for food.

He did help me with my house. He put up a couple of shelves in my living room, making fist- sized holes in my wall. He put in a door stopper that didn't stop the door.

The relationship lasted from the winter of 2000–2001 to the spring of 2002. It faded away until it just ended. Dead. When I look back on that time, I remember how difficult a time it was for me, and how Adam filled some needs. He got me moving toward being on my own. As for the two of us as a couple, it would never have worked.

One highlight of the relationship was that he had a very famous cousin. And we once went to an event for his cousin, where I met such people as Joan Baez, Kris Kristofferson, and Robin Williams.

Chapter 16

The Soul Mate (2002)

*"I can't see myself ever getting married again," said Noah
on that July afternoon. We had just had our first date—
lunch and a walk around downtown Petaluma, California.
It was a great success. We had a second date lined up.
However, one should always listen to what someone says
and proceed with caution, if at all.
Was I ready to get married?
Hell, no.
My divorce would not be final for years.
But I knew I wanted to remarry. Soon.*

I met Noah through my daughter's high school. He was her teacher for a
one-semester course. I had seen him briefly at the school a couple of times.
My daughter was going through our divorce at the time, and she missed
school one day because we had to go to court. She rarely missed school,
and Noah was kind enough to ask where she was. When she told him,
he offered a friendly ear to listen. I appreciated that. He even attended
a performance of hers to which she had invited her teachers. I didn't see
him, but she did. However, he was gone before either of us talked to him.

The couple of times I saw Noah at school, I thought he was pretty cute.
I was "single" again and anxious to pair up since my breakup with Adam
only months before. I asked my daughter if Noah was married. She didn't
know and said she couldn't believe I thought he was "cute." She asked

around and told me she thought he might be divorced. I was interested in finding out more about Noah, but I waited until the school year was over.

It was June 2002. I finally sent Noah an e-mail at his school address (easy to find online at the school website) with my resume, telling him that I was looking for work and that he seemed very connected and active in the community. It was sort of an excuse, but I *was* looking for work, and from what I found out about him online he was very active in education and in the community as a whole.

I had been working as a part time contract editor for a telecom company since 1997, but a few years later the telecom boom collapsed, and people were getting laid off left and right. I wasn't laid off because I was not a direct employee. However, eventually, at the beginning of 2001, I was not renewed. I had not worked since then.

Noah wrote back saying I had an impressive resume, but he wasn't sure if he could do anything about suggesting a job. I went out on a limb here, telling him I appreciated his kindness to my daughter when she needed it. I told him he seemed like a nice man, and I asked if he was married. Yup, I really did that.

He wrote back and said that his marriage had ended a year ago. I replied that mine had as well. He also told me that he was going to be a grandfather for the first time. I must have sneaked in my phone number at some point because shortly thereafter, he called me. Thank goodness those were the days when I still answered the phone.

We had a nice phone conversation, mostly small talk. After we hung up, I thought to myself, *Well, I got him to call me, but he didn't ask me out. What do I do now?* I thought I should probably just wait, something I would likely not have the patience to do at this point. He did call again, and this time we made arrangements to meet for lunch.

It took a lot of work to find a day when we were both free. I was Supermom at the time with lots of driving duties to my kids' activities. They were fourteen and fifteen at the time. There was skating, and dancing, and drums, and guitar, and karate. Noah was busy too. He was working and was also involved in civic and volunteer activities.

We set the lunch date about three weeks out, planning to meet at a downtown restaurant. When I walked in and said I was meeting someone, they showed me to the table where Noah was already seated. He stood, so gentlemanly. I was surprised when he said he didn't remember ever seeing me before at school and had had no idea what I looked like.

Two things stand out in my memory about that lunch: I choked on my iced tea, which was completely embarrassing. And Noah had a stain on his bluish gray pullover. Such a thing might bother me now, but it didn't back then. I remember exactly what I wore that day too. It was a sleeveless print dress that I wore and wore for years after that date. Not long ago, I finally got rid of it after saving it for so long. And I was wearing a pair of low-heeled white shoes that were very uncomfortable. And they are long gone.

After lunch we walked around town; oh, yes, my feet were killing me, but I didn't say anything! I didn't want to ruin the good time we were having. He told me he had been separated from his wife for a year—the same amount of time as I had been separated—and his divorce was to become final soon. Mine took another five or six years! His kids were all grown, so there were no custody or child support issues there. He had waited to leave until his wife got retrained and could get a job and support herself.

We were sitting and talking on a bench when it became time for me to go deliver the kids somewhere. He asked me to go to the art museum on Friday evening (it was now Wednesday) for a special event for museum members. Of course I said yes.

On Friday evening Noah picked me up, and we went to dinner on our way to the museum in San Francisco. When he got up to go to the men's room, I thought to myself, *I have died and gone to heaven. He is the perfect man.*

I adored Noah. We continued to see each other every other weekend, when my children were at their dad's. We spoke on the phone about every other day, although I would have preferred every day. He was great to my kids—asking them if they needed money to buy me a Mother's Day gift—and we began to do some things as a family.

Things went along really well into the fall. My kids were with their dad that Thanksgiving, and I spent it with Noah and his family, a few hours from where we lived. It was that weekend, while we were out walking, that he said to me, "Since I met you, for the first time I can imagine getting married again." Months later he said he didn't remember ever saying that. But he did. That Chanukah he bought me a pair of sapphire and diamond earrings.

We spent Christmas together too—his family and me and my children. And we spent New Year's Eve at one of our favorite local restaurants. That was the last time I ever went out for New Year's Eve.

Not Quite So Perfect

Although things were great with Noah, they weren't. He tried very hard not to fall in love, although it seemed to me that he loved me. Sometimes. He talked about his future with his children and grandchildren, which he was just starting to have. We would often drive by a certain house he loved. He imagined himself living there with his grandchildren. I never seemed to be part of his plans. That was hurtful. And no. He would never tell me he loved me. And I hadn't said it to him, not wanting to be the first to say it and probably not hearing it said back.

We were once at an event with some acquaintances of his. One of them asked Noah what he was going to do during the summer. He talked about spending time with his kids and grandchildren. His friend then asked him, "But what about your beautiful girlfriend?" Unfortunately, it was like that much of the time.

Valentine's Day can be a big disappointment for people who expect too much. People like me. Remember when Alan got me the little penguin holding flowers and I pouted until he threw it and made a hole in the wall? Well, Noah gave me a painting of a bunch of hearts that he had in his house. No card. Just a painting he already owned. I was pretty hurt, and then he was pretty angry. He thought he had done a good job. Nope.

All those things aside, the relationship continued going pretty well. I would plan to tell him I loved him every weekend we spent together, and then I would chicken out. I never told him. Having made it through Valentine's Day, we continued on. May was a good month for us. We had now gone out for about ten months. We went away for a weekend, and he almost told me he loved me. Almost? We were sitting in a restaurant. He told me he loved me in sign language. When I asked about it, he said, "Only the deaf will know." Go figure.

May was great, but by July of 2003—a year into the relationship— things were starting to fall apart. I became increasingly upset that I felt like a low priority in his life. I know that is somewhat true, but I am sure some of it had to do with my perception and my own insecurity.

I became very angry when one Sunday morning he had to leave early to pick up his brother at the airport, and he didn't invite me. I swore at him, and he ran out the door in a huge huff, even leaving his dog behind with me. Later that day I returned the dog, but I didn't see Noah. I would say that was the beginning of the end.

Four days later he called and said he missed me. We got together, but he implied that from now on we would just be friends. Nothing in the relationship, however, seemed to change after that, although I guess we were both angry and resentful. I continued to get mixed messages. He would talk about our future together, but on the other hand, seemed to think we were just friends. I guess he thought we were "just friends" the entire time because that is as far as he wanted it to go. But I certainly thought differently.

It was hard for me to understand what was going on. That summer Noah had a grandchild and then soon after, another grandchild. He told me it would be nice that his grandchildren would grow up knowing me, and that they would consider me a grandmother. And he made references to going away together in the future. I was confused. It sounded to me as if he was picturing a future of some type together.

I figured that once you are in your fifties, you don't need years to figure out how you feel about someone. I started to pressure him and ask why he didn't want to marry me. I know I was in no position to marry again at this point; my divorce didn't become final for years. Although his divorce had become final that summer, he wasn't thinking about marriage. Lots of people remarry a year or two after their divorce. Just not Noah.

By September things were very rocky; by October they were pretty much done. Months before, he had invited me to his daughter's wedding, which was in November. In October he asked me if I still wanted to go since we weren't "together" anymore. If I were not such a fool, I would have said no, but I couldn't bear the thought of us not being together. I decided to go and make a last-ditch effort at this dead relationship.

On the day of the wedding, he showed up at my door with my favorite coffee drink. We went to the wedding, where I figured my only way to get through it was to have a couple of strong drinks, which I did. And I don't drink very much. Since we appeared to be a couple, the photographer asked us to be in a picture together; I hesitated because we weren't a couple any longer, but Noah wanted to do it. I wonder what he did with that picture.

To me, when someone involves you with his family, as he did shortly after the beginning of our relationship, it means they are "serious" about you. When they make plans for the future, to me it means they are "serious" about you. Maybe it was the pressure I put on him, and I just should have waited it out. Maybe I just wasn't the one. Or maybe it was just bad timing.

We had coffee a couple of times after we parted ways. Whenever I suggested we get back together, he acted as if I was going to throw him into a pit of alligators. He said he didn't want any relationship at all with anyone.

Two years after we broke up, by chance I ended up working at the high school for the summer. He was there as well. I had gotten my teaching credential the year before at his urging. And I did need a job to support myself and my kids. I would go to his office at the end of each day and talk to him, but he just wasn't interested in anything besides a friendship. I can't even describe how much I loved that man, how much I wanted to be with him, and how devastated I was.

I have never really gotten over Noah. For many years after our breakup, I would look into every restaurant or public place in town to make sure he wasn't there before I went in, because we lived in the same town, and he had been there pretty much his entire life. My daughter and her then-boyfriend spotted him once with a woman, but they assured me she "wasn't nearly as pretty" as I was.

Years Later

In 2008, I was having coffee with an acquaintance who had worked with Noah several years before I dated him. She told me she heard he had recently gotten married. Because I was involved in a new relationship—which turned out to be three or four dates and was over—I didn't completely fall apart at this news. And it turns out that a close friend of mine knew his new wife from many years ago through her children. It was really hard to get away from Noah and the memories of Noah.

In 2010, when I started writing books and having bookstore appearances, Noah would come and buy a book. He was pleasant and supportive and always asked about my kids. A couple of times his wife was with him. The first time his wife was there, he talked with me without introducing us; she was talking to someone nearby that she knew. More recently, they both talked to me, and it wasn't easy. In fact, after that, I e-mailed him and asked him to please not come to any more events because he had "ruined my life." I am pretty sure he thought that was absurd of me to say, but there is definitely an element of truth to it. I haven't had a serious relationship since Noah, and we broke up in 2003. He ruined it for me because I can't find another "Noah."

I have moved to the other coast, so there is no danger of running in to Noah at this point. But he does e-mail now and then. Before I moved, he suggested coffee a time or two, but I just knew I couldn't do it.

Some people I knew who worked with Noah years before I knew him didn't like him. They said he had a terrible temper. But he was generous to me and my children. He always gave money to any homeless person we passed in the street. I had never seen anyone do that before. He had great respect for women and always told me I was "remarkable." He was always great to his family. I still think Noah should have been my second husband. But he married someone else—so I guess he thought otherwise.

As I look back, I feel bad for my kids. They were young teenagers, and I probably shouldn't have brought Noah—or Adam—into their lives. I probably should have considered them more and not dated for a while after the marriage ended. By the time Noah and I broke up, they were both teenagers with their own lives.

After Noah, it was all downhill.

Chapter 17

The Fix-ups

*"I met this guy at a singles dance," my best friend, Harriet, told me,
"and we were talking, but there was no romance between us.
I think you two might like each other though."*

Harriet and I met in 1995 at an ice rink in California, since both our
daughters were skaters at the time. We commiserated about our marriages. I left mine first. She left hers later. I am still single. She has been
happily remarried for 12 years!

Harriet did a yeoman's job of trying to fix me up three times after
Noah and I broke up. No, none of them worked out.

The Greek God (2004)

When Harriet was single and looking, she told me about Gary Brock,
whom she had met at a single's dance. He was there with a friend of his,
Gary not being the type to attend anything like that. Harriet and Gary
got to talking, although nothing romantic ever happened between them.
She mentioned me to him and told him I was reading a dating book about
bringing back old-fashioned dating habits. The book was called *All the
Rules: Time-tested Secrets for Capturing the Heart of Mr. Right*. Since Gary
was a modern man, he was fascinated and told her he would like to talk to
me about it. She told me he was a nice-looking guy, and she thought we
might like each other—despite the book I was reading. So, shortly thereafter, Harriet invited both of us to her birthday party.

Gary lived an hour and a half away from us, and I was already at the party when a tall blond man who looked like a Greek god walked in. Harriet was right. Gary was very, very handsome. He was also about eight years younger than I. We started to talk, and he asked me if I wanted to go out to lunch, his treat. He said it would probably be the only time anything would be his treat—referring to the book I had been reading where the man always pays—so I should probably take advantage of it. I did, and we went out for Chinese food. We had a nice time talking, and he invited me to his house for "tea." The following weekend I drove down to his house, where he performed a tea ceremony, and I had about eighteen cups of tea. Then he made a salad to wash it down with.

Gary was, however, completely heartbroken over the recent demise of a long-term relationship. He was still sleeping on the living room floor because he couldn't bear to sleep where they had slept. He was incredibly distrustful and fearful of women at this point.

I liked him, but I wasn't that interested in a relationship with him. Handsome as he was, he wasn't really my type. I recall that he had a burning incense stick stuck in the drain of his shower. I thought that was a little odd.

Gary and I communicated for a while, but I never saw him again. His distrust of women led to some disagreements over the phone about love and relationships. I sent him a music CD of someone he said he liked, and he told me he was terrified of me and was returning it. I guess it was something I said, although I never figured out what. As far as I know, he is still single, but then so am I.

The Artist (2005)

Next, Harriet fixed me up with Ed, an artist who lived across the street from her. Unlike Gary, Ed was several years older than I, but he was a good-looking guy—and who doesn't love an artist? We went out to hear music. It was right before Harriet remarried, and he asked me if I was going to the wedding—of course I was—and asked if he could be my date. He was not close enough to Harriet to have been invited himself. I didn't even know him, so I kind of laughed it off. A few minutes later, he said his knee hurt, so he had to go home. So much for that.

I found out through Harriet a little later that Ed had started dating someone we both knew slightly; he was with her for several years until a few years ago. Shortly after that I saw Ed on the dating site I was on; he actually wrote to me, but apparently didn't recognize who I was and that we had already gone out once. I knew who he was, and I wrote back to him, not realizing he had no idea who I was. That communication stopped there.

Not too long after that, Ed was having an open house for his art. He sent me an invitation; I don't know how I got on his mailing list. So I went over there with Harriet. Since we had gone out that one time, and then had communicated a little on the dating site, I assumed when I went to see his art—and since I was with Harriet, who had fixed us up in the first place—he would know who I was. Nope. He had no idea. It was rather insulting that he still did not remember me! Harriet and I both assumed at that point that he knew who I was. However, somewhere during our conversation with him, it became obvious he had no idea.

A few years later, I was at a small live music event, and I saw someone sitting there I thought might be him. A woman at the next table got up and started talking to him, and then they danced. I was dying to know if that was him; he had aged quite a bit. Of course, he showed no sign of recognizing me. When she returned to her seat, I asked the woman what his name was. She said she had known him for years, but she didn't remember his name. All she remembered was that he was an artist. I asked, "Is his name Ed?"

She said, "Yes, that's what it is!" I had no real reason to go up and say anything to him, so I didn't. He probably would not remember me anyway.

The Rude Man (2005)

Harriet's third try to fix me up was even more unsuccessful than the first two, through no fault of hers. All three men were nice looking and intelligent, and they apparently had nothing wrong with them. This time she invited a man who worked with her husband to meet us at an outdoor bar and restaurant. It was just the three of us. She told me that Lawrence was very nice looking, although he was several years older than I was. And he was a pretty nice-looking guy with pretty silver hair. And so freaking rude I couldn't believe it.

He talked to Harriet, but he completely ignored me and seemed to look at me with scorn. And that was that. He did find someone, whom he has been with for years, and she seems nice. Before I moved away to Florida, I would see them from time to time because they are friends with Harriet and her husband. I still could not stand to be in the same room with him. I would give him a dirty look and leave the room. I am sure he doesn't remember or realize how rude he was.

The Musician (2017)

My last fix-up was a few years ago. I was still in California at the time. Deb, a writer friend of mine, told me she thought her boyfriend's closest friend and I might hit it off. Her boyfriend and Norm were in the same band. She invited us both to dinner with her and her longtime boyfriend. Norm was nice, but there was just no attraction. He was a little too quiet for my taste. We did become friends though. I went to see Norm play at a small event not too long afterwards. We keep in touch on social media, and when I still lived in California, we went out for lunch as friends a few times. I also invited him to my parties where I would invite several musician friends to jam together. Norm is one hell of a good musician. It just wasn't a love connection.

Chapter 18

Online and Off the Wall

"Your yard is disgusting and full of dog poop."

"And now I am with someone who has a flat stomach."

Those are excerpts from an e-mail I received after several dates with Joe, an actor. He was an online "find." Between 2001, when I left my marriage, and 2019, when I moved to Florida, I was off and on dating sites between those fix-ups and dates with men I met in the real world. I met a whole lot of men online, most of them fine, some of them quite "memorable." These relationships lasted anywhere from a coffee date to a few months. But nothing stuck at all.

Bowling Man (2004)

I met Marty early in my online dating career. It was 2004, about a year after my breakup with Noah. I was still brokenhearted, and my standards were pretty low. Some of the men I would go out to meet, I pretty much knew I wouldn't like from their profiles or pictures, but I went anyway. Anything to take my mind off Noah. Anything for even the slightest possibility of "love."

Marty was not very attractive to me, as I recall. Nor was he very interesting. He owned a local bowling alley. He was from my hometown, and we went out exactly once—to dinner. At the end of our date, he said to me, "You are nice in kind of a morose way." I know I was still getting over Noah, but I truly don't think I was morose on this date. And if I was, it was because I wasn't liking him much. He was pretty humorless. Never saw him again.

But there is more to this story. I began teaching seventh grade English in a middle school where I lived shortly after that date. Coincidentally, I had one of Noah's nephews in my class. I knew ahead of time I was going to have Barry in my class, and I had e-mailed Noah about it. I thought it would be difficult for me, and I was going to ask that he be moved to another class, but Noah thought it would be fine. Ultimately it was, and Barry was a fine student.

Not long after the school year began, one of the girls in class raised her hand. I acknowledged her, and she shouted out, from her desk in the back of the room, to the entire class, "My father says you know him." I thought about it for a few seconds and put two and two together. From their matching last names, I knew this was Bowling Man's daughter. Then I remembered that in his online dating profile photo he was with a little girl.

I didn't quite know what to say. Stalling for time, I asked what his name was, and then I said, "Yes, I met him once." That was true. I did meet him once. She then added, still shouting to the whole class, "My father says you went out with him." I replied, again, "I met your father once." I wanted to add, "And I didn't like him very much," but of course I didn't.

It happened that this student, Maddie, was in the same class as Noah's nephew, Barry, and they sat close to one another. A few days after the incident with Maddie, I was going around the room checking homework. One of the boys who sat near both Maddy and Barry, said to me, "So you went out with her father *and* with his uncle?" Embarrassing moment.

Since I had gone out with Noah for a while, I guess Barry mentioned that I had dated his uncle to some of his classmates. Pretty normal thing to do. I had met Barry once or twice when I was dating his uncle. So, I said, "I went out with his uncle." I didn't mention Bowling Man, Maddie's dad.

Thankfully, I don't think the entire class heard this. An unfortunate coincidence in a seventh-grade class.

The Genius (2005)

Another of the early men I met online was Ben Bank. His last name wasn't really Bank, but I called him that because he worked part time at a bank—and since his last name was similar to Bank, he called himself that as well. Our first date was at a nice pizza restaurant. I remember thinking how handsome he was, and that I never date handsome men like that. He had very long hair—really nice long hair—and a nicely chiseled face. He seemed quite amiable and gentlemanly that first date. We ended up going out about a half-dozen times over a few months. Ben was not highly educated, but he claimed to be a genius. He was very well read and a bit eccentric—and, intelligent as I am, much of what he said went right over my head. He had some quotes that he would say over and over again, from various beat writers, among them, Charles Bukowski, whom he talked about often. In addition to his part time job at the bank, he was a photographer and had once had a cable television show.

We once went to a birthday party where Ben was hired as the photographer. The party was for the husband of a dominatrix. I had never met a dominatrix before, but she seemed nice enough, despite her outfit.

Ben was into drugs and alcohol. When we dated, he drove, but eventually he told me he had no license because it had been suspended. Why on earth did I ever go anywhere with him in his car after he told me that? He carried around a small bottle of peppermint liqueur in his glove box that he would drink from. While we were dating, I once saw him somewhere meeting another woman. Looking for something "better"? Over the several months that we dated, we really didn't see each other terribly regularly.

I saw Ben several times after we stopped dating, usually at outdoor music events because he loved to "dance," and was quite a show off. He ended up dating someone for years after we stopped seeing each other. I didn't really know her, but we had a couple of mutual friends. Ben and his lady seemed very similar, but they eventually broke up. When I look back, I would never date him now. Totally not for me. It was a physical attraction mostly. And his eccentricity amused me.

The Actor (2005)

Joe, the actor, and I went out several times. He was decent looking, but again, looking back, why was I with this person? I recall two of our few dates. On one date, I was at his house listening to music and eating hummus and bread. He seemed like a nice host to me. Then I remember our last "date." He was at my house. We had not slept together on our first several dates. Then we did, and he indicated when he left that he wasn't going to call me again. I was livid and felt used.

I e-mailed him to tell him how I felt. In his e-mail back to me he told me he was disgusted because I had a yard full of dog poop (I had two dogs at the time) and now he was dating a woman who had a flat stomach. What a guy. Okay, I might have had dog poop in my yard, which was very easy to see because I had concrete and no grass. I did eventually pick up the poop on my own poop-pickup schedule. And as far as the "flat-stomach" comment, that surprised me. I wasn't fat, and my stomach was always pretty flat, even though it might not be so much now. Hey, I had had two C-sections!

Hatman (2006)

And then there was Hatman. His name was actually Diego. He was very cute. We met online. I am not sure where he lived, but he traveled from one county fair to the next during fair season selling hats. Our relationship lasted the amount of time the fair was in my county, a couple of weeks. I don't know what his transportation situation was, but he used me to run errands. He asked me to go buy him some mirrors for his fair booth, and I used to pick him up from the fair to see him, but at least my daughter and I got free hats out of the deal. Back then, before Apple Pay and whatever other new payment systems were popular, lots of his hat customers paid cash. He would keep wads of cash in his socks. Hard to forget that. When he went along to the next fair, which was a couple of hours away, he invited me to come down "if I wanted to," but the invitation seemed pretty lackluster, and I never did. Then he told me he had found someone at his next fair. Easy come, easy go.

Raw Food Man (2006)

This man was one of the weirdest people I have ever gone out with. He invited me for dinner at a mutually convenient restaurant that I had never been to. This was years ago, and I was much younger, so I was going out with men who were younger. He claimed on his profile to be 47. I was surprised because in person he looked quite a bit older than that. When he walked into the restaurant, I saw that he was carrying something, and I figured it was a briefcase. I saw later that it was a board he used for his bad back.

He also had thinning gray hair, glasses, and the worst turkey neck I had ever seen on someone his age. This is all-important because it doesn't quite fit in with the rest of the story.

I looked at the menu, and being one of those women who is always on or off some diet or another, I debated whether to go all out with something fattening or to "be good." I started talking to him about what I was considering ordering. He said he wasn't going to order anything because his stomach had been bothering him. I told him he should have canceled if he wasn't going to eat anything. He said maybe he would get something later.

So, I ordered. Although appearing to the contrary, he claimed to be quite fit and athletic; he had once coached a world-famous tennis star— and had the pictures on his dating profile to prove it. And then it began. Once I ordered, he told me that the only food we should eat is a lot of raw fat. I will never forget that. He told me how he had written an article about it, but it was too "difficult" for most people to understand. He said his son lived with his ex-wife, and unfortunately his mother fed him all kinds of unhealthy food. He tried to give his son healthy foods when he was with him, but he wasn't always cooperative, and my date felt sorry about this.

Eventually he ordered some raw beef and some tomato slices. He continued to drone on about how brilliant he was and what a fine specimen of health he was—even telling me that his prostate was that of a young man's. I sat there and wondered why he had a board to help his bad back, a terrible turkey neck, bad eyes, and unhealthy-looking hair if he was such a healthy specimen. He didn't look healthy at all.

The conversation turned to our kids, and I showed him some pictures on my phone of my son and daughter. He kept saying how beautiful my daughter was until it became very creepy indeed.

I will never forget his parting words at the end of our date. He said, "I have given you the very best gift of all today, the gift of knowledge." No, I never saw him again. As a matter of fact, this was one time when I couldn't imagine how anyone had ever married this man, and how anyone would ever date him more than once. I don't know what happened to him. And I don't remember his name.

Pomegranate Seed Man (2007)

This first meeting was a little risky on my part. Roger lived in the next county, so we arranged to meet halfway. He had planned a picnic. When I drove up to our meeting place, he was already there, and his trunk was packed with food for our picnic. He asked if I just wanted to leave my car there and go with him in his car. I would never do that now. I had never met this man before. But I agreed to leave my car there, in some parking lot, and go with him. I was lucky.

We never went for a picnic at all. Turns out he was house-sitting a very fancy house on the San Francisco Bay in a very fancy town, where the houses were worth upwards of ten million. I guess it was a nice house, but definitely not my taste. It seemed very dark and eerie inside.

We brought the food in from his trunk and had an indoor picnic. After eating, he suggested we take a walk. For some reason, I decided to leave my purse, which held my cell phone. I don't think I would go for a walk in the evening with a stranger without a cell phone now! He didn't want to take the house key with us, so he left it where the owner of the house had left it for him, under a vase that sat on a ledge on the porch. We went for a short walk and by the time we got back, it was dark.

He reached under the vase to get the key to the house, and it fell down several feet into the bushes. We had no phones. We had no flashlight. He crawled into the bushes for a while looking for the key, but it was dark and he couldn't find it. There were no neighbors around. We decided to walk to the police station to see if someone there could maybe help us out. It was a very small town, and it was walking distance to the tiny police station.

It was not really late, but it was after dark. We got to the police station, and it was closed. Yes, closed. Maybe there was an emergency number posted, but then we had no phone. Luckily we saw a police car on our walk back and flagged it down. The two police in the car drove us to the house, and they went looking for the key. Since they had flashlights, they were able to locate the key. We got into the house. Saved.

But that wasn't enough excitement for the evening to get me to leave. Once we got into the house, he decided to feed me pomegranate seeds for dessert, I assume because they have the reputation of being an aphrodisiac. He became obnoxiously forward, and I was not at all interested. I was a little angry at his being so irresponsible as to lose the key in the bushes, and I just didn't really like him. He became angry as well. I fought him off for a while, and then I told him to just drive me back to my car.

I was lucky that he agreed to drive me back to my car, since he was angry I had rebuffed him. And it was a good thing since I had little idea of where my car was parked. I got into my car with great relief and started to drive home. Within a few minutes my cell phone rang.

It was Roger, saying he was sorry, and could we try it again, since he thought we were right for each other. I said No. He called another time or two while I was driving home. Still, No. End of story.

The Games Man (2008)

I call Lawrence Mendelson The Games Man because he claimed to be the "father of video games," having invented one of the first games. Technically, according to Google, his title is actually close to that. He was also a championship bridge player and a physician. We went out several times, and then he disappeared for a while. Then he called again, and we went out a few more times. His behavior was very odd. He would make plans for us that implied we were going to be together forever. If I mentioned something I would be doing or someplace I would be going—probably involving one of my kids—he would say, "Of course, I will be going along to that. " And then he would disappear again. He did claim to be divorced and have two children, which I believe was the truth. His kids were a couple of hours away, so he was often off seeing his kids . . . or at least that was his excuse.

Nothing much romantic happened between the two of us, although he was my type and he was interesting. The last time I saw him, we went to a local restaurant with a game room where people would play bridge. He didn't play that night, but he went in and seemed to know everyone there.

Here is the finale to this dating story. I was teaching school at the time I was seeing him. A few days after that final dinner out with him, at morning break, I opened my classroom closet to check my cell phone. There were a couple of texts from him. They were X-rated, the likes of which I have never seen in a text, about things that never happened between us. I couldn't figure out if he was imagining that these things *did* happen, or that he was sending the message to the wrong person, which I thought was more likely. I did confront him about the texts; he apologized and hinted that they were meant for someone else. End of that one.

I did continue to see Lawrence on the online dating site. I think we even connected once, but we never saw each other again, although I wouldn't bet against the fact that he talked about seeing each other again. He was like that.

Menu Man (2009)

Randy was from Carmel, which was a few hours from where I lived in California. It surprised me that he was willing to come up and take me out to dinner in my area. He was probably used to driving around the area because he was a wine salesperson. He knew about wine and enjoyed conversing about it with the sommelier. We went to one of the nicer—and pricier—restaurants in town. He ordered a glass of wine for himself and one for me. Then another. He also ordered some appetizers, oh, maybe three or four. Then, a bottle of wine. And another. And another. Bear in mind that two glasses of wine is my limit.

Then he ordered our entrees. Three, maybe four of them. Randy was interested in sampling most of the wines and most of the food. I had never seen anyone order so much food. Much of it was "weird" things I had never had like bone marrow. And of course he drank most of the wine. It was a very fun evening, but I will never forget the amount of food he ordered. I don't even know how much the check was, obviously at least several hundred dollars. We made fuzzy plans to meet again, but we never did. The distance was greater than the attraction.

Whoops! Guy (2019)

A couple of years ago, I had an odd experience on the dating site. I received an e-mail from a person who lived in my city and was a writer like me. The dating site now likes you to use your real first name, so this person said his name was Christopher. I, however, don't use my real name. I was using some initials at the time.

I looked at Christopher's profile and he seemed OK, if not a bit pretentious. His picture was a little blurry, and nothing noteworthy—and he had only one photo. But his e-mail turned me off. In the first paragraph, when he expounded about his writing, he said that his humor writing was "very well regarded." In his second paragraph, he said he really didn't trust anyone to give an opinion about his writing. In the third paragraph he said he thought I would find his profile much better written than most. I assume he was responding to the part of my profile where I say that although I am a writer, I find it difficult to write a profile about myself. Because his e-mail indicated to me that I probably would not like this man, I didn't write back at all.

In a few days, he wrote to me again, this time only one paragraph. He ended his e-mail by saying that it appeared as if I had "more than one creative thought in my head," and added that I was pretty. I didn't exactly take the "more than one creative thought" comment as the compliment it was likely intended to be. I answered this e-mail.

I told Christopher that I didn't answer his initial e-mail because of the bragging throughout, which really didn't appeal to me. I added that I didn't consider his backhanded compliment about my having more than one creative thought in my head as a compliment at all. I also said that I was indeed very intelligent and well educated. Snarky? Maybe. People tell me I have an "Eastern edge" because I am originally from Boston.

Christopher wrote back a couple of paragraphs telling me about my anger issues and recommending that I take those anger issues to a therapist. Then he signed his full name along with his advanced degree.

Turns out that I had been editing Christopher's writing for about five years. I had never met him, so I didn't recognize his photo. Since his main occupation is not writing, I didn't connect his name and the fact he was a writer with the person whose work I had been editing.

Christopher writes short pieces, mostly political. His field is not politics, but he is interested and knowledgeable about it. In fact, he often would e-mail me just to talk about current events. He is actually a psychologist. Christopher was referred to me by a mutual acquaintance several years ago when he was looking for an editor. When I began to edit for him, he lived in another city; he had recently moved to mine, but I never met him in person.

So now I knew who Christopher was, but he didn't recognize me online, because I was not using my first name. I wrote back to him, using not the dating site e-mail but his regular e-mail—which I had because we had been working together. I asked if he was the same Christopher who wrote me those e-mails on the dating site (I knew he was), and that I would recommend he find a new editor. Most appalling to me was that statement that he didn't trust anyone to evaluate his writing. All the time I had been his editor, he was very appreciative of my comments (which were many), very nice to me, seemingly pleased with my work—and he always paid, on time if not ahead of time.

He wrote back with his tail between his legs as much as possible for him, saying he didn't recognize it was me, and that he was "sorry it had to end this way."

Christopher was involved in another coincidence. While I was still editing for him, he had written to me saying he had an e-mail exchange with an editor who lived close to me and whom I might know. He said he wasn't looking for an editor, but someone to help with publishing. Christopher was unhappy with their exchange, and said he told the gentleman he already had an editor and wasn't looking for that. He claimed that this editor had reached out to him looking for work. I told Christopher I did indeed know this person, who was actually a friend of mine. Christopher said they wouldn't be communicating any longer. I talked to my editor friend, and he said he had no idea what Christopher wanted from him. I don't really know who reached out to whom. Small world.

And Many More

Many of the men I met online remain memorable. Some of the time it was only coffee or a drink or lunch or dinner. Sometimes there were a couple of dates, or a few, or maybe more.

- The five-times married astrologer who did my chart, which I still have.
- The guy who looked like a blow-up doll my daughter used for a skating routine prop.
- The prison guard who was nice on the phone, but as I suspected, wasn't a match.
- The one I met right after Noah, whose name was also Noah, and who knew Noah.
- The one whom my friend met online; she dragged me along on her date, and I ended up with him for the evening, after she gave up on him and went home.
- The bitter one whose main interest was being angry at his ex-wife, calling her crazy.
- The guy whom I had seen at some ballroom dances who wore pastel and smelled bad.
- The engineer whose family had been involved in a very newsworthy murder.
- The depressed man who became claustrophobic in the small restaurant and had to leave.
- The one who wore a purple ribbon in his hair.
- The one who bragged because he had a "neutral accent," and I had a slight (very slight and really unnoticeable) Boston accent.
- The one who told me he was my "boyfriend for the weekend," who was interested in nothing except sex.
- The one I scared away by talking too much about politics.

- The man who brought flowers and invited me to his house for dinner for our next date, and then the next day cancelled. There was someone else.

- The man I met once and then years later met again online and went out with once again; it still didn't work.

- The man who managed the candy store; should have stuck with that one!

Chapter 19

Just Friends

*"I would be honored to have coffee with you," Evan replied in an e-mail.
I thought this could be the start of a great relationship.*

You may ask if I have any male friends after all this dating. I have never had a real male buddy like some women do, whom they hang around with a lot. But I have male friends. Of course, there are the "friends" on social media, some of whom I haven't ever met in person, but I won't count those for now. I don't really have any male friends at all where I live now. I have been in this house for nearly a year now, and all of that time we have been in a pandemic, so it is hard to make new friends. But I had male friends in California.

Male friends seem to come from three different sources, and I have male friends from each of the three.

1. Sometimes men you have had romantic relationships with become friends, generally if it ends mutually with no one getting a broken heart. Or maybe you can be friends after a while, when you have healed, and perhaps one or both of you have found other partners. Many people remain friends with ex-lovers and ex-husbands. I wouldn't say I am exactly friends with most of my exes.

2. Sometimes you run into a man at work or at an activity and you become friends. Either there isn't the attraction to make the relationship go any further, or perhaps they are married or gay or both. It is best in these cases if neither person wants anything more than friendship.

Sometimes you have dated a few times, and you both find that it is better as a friendship.

3. Sometimes you acquire male friends because they are attached to a female friend. Often a female friend will get married, or is already married, and you become friends with her husband or boyfriend. This isn't exactly the same as when you are a couple and you become "friends" with another couple, so you socialize as couples. This is more of a threesome deal. There are those women who like to include their men in the female-female friendship. They are friends mostly by virtue of being there. If you don't like the husband or boyfriend, and the friend always includes him, that could be a problem.

When I think about male friends, I think about these guys.

Juan (2002)

I haven't seen or heard from Juan in a long time. First, he moved out of California and then I did. Juan wasn't a really close friend. And neither of us ever had any romantic feelings about the other—as far as I know. I first saw Juan when he was playing live music in my tap dance class in the late nineties. We usually didn't have live musicians, but for this particular dance we had a live drummer. I noticed that Juan was really nice looking, but I don't think I ever spoke to him all the weeks he played drums for us.

A short while later, after the class had ended, I saw an article about him in my local paper. Since the dance class was a few towns away, I didn't realize he lived where I did. I also discovered that he was primarily an actor. I contacted him, since I always thought he was cute. Juan was trying to further his career as an actor, and I was trying to get my book-writing business going. So we made a deal to meet for coffee maybe once a month to spur each other on. Nothing romantic ever transpired between us, although we were both single.

Juan seemed to have many female friends, but I was never aware of him dating anyone. He had been married and had one grown child. We met for coffee until he moved to southern California to get his acting career going. He had some luck there, but ultimately decided to move to Oregon to be near his young grandchildren. He stopped in to his hometown before he moved to Oregon, and a friend had a going away party for him. That is the last time I saw Juan.

Max (2008)

Max was the 9th grade prom date who I thought for the next forty years had asked me to the prom on a bet.

We reconnected on social media when we were both contacted about our fortieth high school reunion. I had not been to a high school reunion in twenty or twenty-five years, and I had attended only one. When they were planning the fortieth, the organizers were connecting with people and finding them on social media. I was in California by then, and Max was still in New England, but had long ago moved out of Massachusetts, where we had gone to school.

Max and I became friends on social media, and then we started to talk on the phone. He never married, but has been with the same woman for over thirty years. When I went back to Boston to see my daughter about eight years ago, I spent a lovely afternoon with Max. He drove me around the old neighborhood; I got to see the three-story house I had grown up in. It looked so much smaller than it had then, as did the yard. Our old high school was gone, rebuilt in a new location, so Max took me to see that. And he drove me downtown, which was still recognizable in some parts. Even Cal's News, where I used to walk after high school nearly every day to see if *Billboard Magazine* had come yet, was still there. And there was a restaurant I went to all the time with my mother and grandmother that was long gone, but the faded picture of a lobster was still there on the side of the yellow brick building. Lobster? Yes, it was New England after all.

During that visit, Max and I went out to lunch at the same Chinese restaurant we went to after the prom. I was shocked it was still there. How many restaurants last for fifty years? I had a really fun day with Max. And speaking of reunions, the fiftieth occurred right after I moved from California to Florida. Since it was a big reunion, and I was now on the same coast as Massachusetts, I went, and so did Max and his lady, so I got to meet her. Although I think Max is a really nice guy, we wouldn't have been a good match. He is a sports nut, as is his girlfriend; I am pretty uninterested in sports.

Max and I still speak on the phone now and then, and we communicate regularly on social media. He is a good guy.

Leo (2011)

I met Leo at an art class we took for several weeks in 2011. There were only about eight people in the class, and Leo and I were around the same age. I thought he looked interesting. I knew I was single, but I didn't know if Leo was. Another woman in the class told me it was obvious that Leo liked me. I said I thought he was married, as he often used the pronoun *we*. She said lots of people use the pronoun *we*. (I wasn't so sure about that one.) Turns out he was indeed married. Leo is a great guy, He is an attorney, a fine chef, a great artist, a performing musician, and one of the most intelligent people I have ever met.

Leo and I met for coffee a couple of times. The first time we met, we hugged, and I told him I wished he weren't married. I eventually met his wife, who is a lovely woman. I invited them to several of my parties, where he played music. Now that I have moved, I see Leo on social media. I have asked his advice on matters of the heart on occasion because I really trust him, and I consider him a friend.

Norm (2017)

Norm was one of those fix-ups I had. We liked each other, but there was no romantic interest. Before I moved away, we met for coffee or for lunch a few times, and we still talk on social media. And I always invited him to my parties where he would join in with the other musician friends I had, like Leo. We also had good political discussions. The friend who fixed us up tells me he has a girlfriend now, so I am happy for him.

Evan (2017)

I met Evan at a book event, as we are both authors, a few years ago. I thought he was really handsome and really nice. We talked most of the day, but I never saw him after that. He belonged to the writing club I belonged to, but he never attended the meetings. A year later, I saw there was going to be a special event at the writing club. I wasn't going to go until I saw a flyer that said he was participating. I decided to go, although I figured someone who was that handsome and nice was probably not available. I looked him up on social media, and we connected on Facebook or Instagram. There were photos of him with a woman, although I guess it could have been anyone at any time.

Since Evan rarely attended meetings, he didn't know many of the people at the event. So when I walked up to him, I got a big hug, and we ended up talking for most of the afternoon. He told a writer friend of mine that he "loved" me, but in the casual sense of loving what I posted on social media. Once again, at the end of the day, we went our separate ways.

I started investigating him more on social media and found a video of a writing talk he had given. I decided we were meant to be. He was a feminist and a poet, and we loved the same music, I discovered.

I had a copy of his book, so I thought that topic might be a good excuse to e-mail him. If you see a pattern here of my investigating and thinking up excuses to e-mail men, so do I. I think I missed my calling in life.

I e-mailed and told him I was about to start reading his book. To tell you the truth, I started reading it, and it isn't a genre I generally read. I got totally lost, and I didn't finish it.

He answered my e-mail with a friendly, short one. I decided I was going to take further action and ask him out for coffee. He lived about an hour away from me and has two jobs in addition to writing, so he is pretty busy. I e-mailed him and asked him out for coffee; he said he would be "honored" to have coffee with me. In fact, he said he had tickets for a concert the next day and invited me to go with him. I was quite surprised he would be looking for someone to go with him so last minute. He seemed like the type of guy who had many women—even if they were just friends—to choose from.

Ultimately, I didn't go. I had plans with my son, and I wasn't going to break them to go with some man last minute. I have learned that lesson, although there was a friend or two who thought I should have gone. He ended up going alone and giving the extra ticket to someone who was in line.

But we did go out shortly after that. We went out a few times. Our dates were always squeezed into weird, short times because of his work schedule. I am self-employed, so my schedule is more flexible. We would go to a museum or have coffee or go to the movies, and always also for a walk. We went out three times that first week. I thought this might be going somewhere. Then, he actually had a real vacation from work—and he completely disappeared. He went to spend some time with his daughters. Then, when it was time for him to return to work, he tried to fit me in.

Eventually, I heard from him less and less. He would text now and then. I would text back. We had had a few kisses on the cheek, but that is it. He was always very nice. We were still communicating when I took a two-week vacation. He texted and was anxious to get together when I got back. I didn't hear from him until I had been back for nearly a week. We went to a movie, and that was the last time I had a "date" with him.

He used his busyness as an excuse, but I am smart enough to know that when you are interested enough in someone, there are no excuses. You make the time. The first week or two that we went out, he attempted to make the time. Then he didn't. I was hurt and felt insulted that I was so far down his list. I e-mailed him and told him how I felt. He replied that he realized he had "blown" it with me. I told him it was okay (it wasn't really), but he didn't try to rectify anything, and he got more distant. He claims he is just too busy for a relationship. He said his last girlfriend broke up with him because he was too busy.

But this chapter is about friends, not relationships. And Evan and I were much better off as friends. I invited him to my "legendary" music parties. And since I moved away, we have remained in touch by text and social media. I would say we are friends, although long distance now. And when I visited California last year, I did see him. He is another one of the good guys.

Chapter 20

You Can't Go Home Again

"I was thinking that what happened between us was 'just a flirtation,'
but I knew it was really more than that."
I read Peter's e-mail again and again,
and I couldn't stop being a little angry because of course,
I was sure it was more than that—
even though all evidence was to the contrary.

We have all read the stories about couples who were high school sweethearts and broke up for some reason. Maybe they went away to colleges in different parts of the country. Maybe one or both of their parents disapproved of the relationship. Maybe they tried to stay together, but the distance got in the way, or they grew apart. They eventually lose touch with each other. They marry others and raise a family. Sometimes they divorce; sometimes their spouse dies. Sometimes one or both remains single. Then, they meet again years later, maybe several decades later. Maybe at a high school reunion. Or maybe they have kept track of the other all along.

And they get together and rekindle what they had. They marry, often at an older age, when perhaps they thought they would never find love again. They often claim they never stopped loving each other. Call me a real romantic, but I am a real sucker for these stories. Stories like these have always appealed to me. And I have tried to rekindle a couple of relationships.

Doesn't everyone look up their exes on social media? Sometimes I am just really curious about people, even though I may not want to start a romantic relationship with them. I just want to see where they are and what they are doing.

Sometimes I get bored with my love life, or lack thereof, and decide to investigate my exes. It is so easy now with the internet and social media. Of course, usually I just look up my favorites.

Peter Again (2014)

Peter Mendoza, one of the men I met at work in the early eighties, was never a love relationship because he was married. Nothing ever happened between us except conversations and lunches.

Several years after divorce my in 2001, and likely without any type of relationship at the time, I found Peter on social media and contacted him to ask how he was . . . and to try to see if he was still married. Yes, he was still married. He told me a little bit about what he was doing and that he had moved out of Massachusetts, quite a bit closer to where I was on the West Coast. But since he was still married, that was the end of it.

Then, in 2014—I remember it because it was the year of my daughter's wedding—he sent me a Facebook friend request out of the blue. I probably should have left well enough alone, but I always had a real soft spot for Peter. He was so cute, so nice. So I wrote him a brief message. He had just wanted to connect. I was the one who wrote the note. Because . . . me.

It was an innocent enough message, asking him how he was doing. It took just a couple of messages to get this information: He was separated from his wife, whom, by now, he had been married to for a very long time, and he had three grown children. In the ensuing messages, he revealed that he remembered a lot more about our lunches than I did. I remembered only that he was a writer, I was his editor, and we frequently went to lunch together. I would have been interested in him, but I knew he was married, so I figured he liked me just as a friend. Turns out he remembered what I was wearing during some of our lunches. He remembered being parked in some garage and almost kissing me in the car. I have no recollection of any of that.

Now I had all the information I needed. He had been separated for around six months, so of course I figured he would fall madly in love with me. A safe bet? Of course not. But that is apparently my thing. Unavailable men like my father. The challenge of trying to make them interested in me.

A couple of days after we "discovered" each other, he said he would like to talk on the phone if that was okay with me. He called in a day or two and we spoke for three hours. Soon after that we spoke another couple of times, also for three hours. As a means of communicating, we started to play Words with Friends together on our phones, but we had our own special rules that made it so much more creative and fun. He was really funny and witty, and I really enjoyed that.

He looked up the restaurants near me and told me where he would take me if he were here. I assumed, therefore, that he was interested. He also told me about the only date that he had had since he was separated. He said they hadn't slept together or anything, and that was the last he saw of her.

I probably should have considered that he might go back to his wife. And as time wore on, I probably should have also wondered why we didn't speak on the phone more often, or why he didn't take a trip down to see me. He was in another state, but not that far away. I guess I didn't want to admit he was not as interested as I thought he was. I chose to ignore the red flags.

A few months after we initially made contact, he was invited to a wedding a hundred or so miles from where I live. He was thinking of coming to see me. The bride was someone in his wife's family, and she would be there too, but they were going completely separately. Of course it crossed my mind that it would be nice if he had invited me to go to the wedding with him, but I brushed that thought away. He had a rental car, and the plan was to come see me the day before the wedding and stay one night here in a hotel (I had two extra rooms in my house, but I don't think we ever discussed that.)

He also planned to see some old friends from high school, since he grew up and went to high school in San Francisco, an hour away from me. He would go from where I lived to San Francisco the next day, and then drive on down to the wedding.

We had planned an evening date after he arrived from his long drive. I waited anxiously for the phone call that he was here. It took him a little longer to get to me than he thought it would, but he finally called. He had made reservations at a nice restaurant downtown.

He called when he arrived at the hotel, 15 minutes away from me. I felt disappointed when he asked if I wanted him to pick me up or if I wanted to meet him at the restaurant. It felt less like a date if I had to meet him. So I said I would like to be picked up.

When I opened the door for him, he didn't have that bunch of flowers that I was hoping for. Expectations. We hugged, and he was still just as cute as ever. I wouldn't even kiss him on the cheek. I felt uncomfortable because he was still married. He told me at dinner that he had felt awkward too. I think he was going to kiss me, but he noticed I pulled away.

Dinner was fun, and we loosened up. Although I adored him, I didn't feel all woozy with love. Perhaps I had some sense left.

After dinner we walked around downtown. It was August, so the weather was nice. We listened to some street musicians and then went into a bar I had never been in. I am not really the bar type. It was there that I played darts and shuffleboard for the first time. He taught me how to keep score, and I have a photo or two to commemorate the date. Then, he drove me home.

He had plans to drive to San Francisco the next day to his friends from high school, but we made a date to meet for lunch the next day, before he left for San Francisco, at a local place I suggested. I wonder if he would have come to see me at all if it weren't for those friends in San Francisco .

I have to admit I was a little miffed that he wasn't spending more time with me and seemed pretty anxious to get to his friends in San Francisco. Still no kiss, just a hug, but that was comfortable for me.

It turned out that one of his friends never showed up at all, and I think his time with the other one was cut short because he and his wife had plans. This made me even more annoyed—or should I say rejected—that he ran off to be with them. That was the last time I saw Peter.

After that visit his phone calls and communication ebbed. However, we continued to communicate, and we still played Words with Friends.

The state of his marriage? When we saw each other, he had been separated from his wife for nearly a year. He told me that his wife had divorce papers on the table, but neither of them could bring themselves to do anything with the papers. He had told me a long time ago that he and his wife had been just roommates for decades. That is a common line.

For my birthday, which is in September, a few weeks after our date, I posted on Facebook that my greatest birthday wish was to get flowers from a special someone. Sure enough, flowers arrived from Peter with a card saying, "To a wonderful woman."

You know, I have been called a wonderful woman by a lot of men—all of whom had girlfriends or wives already—or didn't seem interested in me, regardless of how wonderful I might be.

Peter and I continued our mild flirting and online games. I noticed something had changed, and I finally asked him what was up. In December he admitted he was getting ready to move back in with his wife—of course as "roommates." He told me things would really have to change a lot to make the marriage viable. I was upset because he didn't come out and tell me on his own that he was going back to his wife after over a year of separation.

Have I heard from Peter since? He sent me a funny book a few years ago, but I didn't see the card, so I didn't know whom it was from for a while. Then I sent him a birthday e-mail but got no such thing in return.

He e-mailed a couple of times to make sure I was okay when the fires hit California. The last thing he told me about his marriage was that they sold the house and were living in an apartment, so it would be easier to split things if they ended up divorcing. That was a couple of years ago. He doesn't seem to be on any social media any longer, so I haven't communicated with him.

I think of Peter very fondly. He is one of the men I probably would have run off with if he had asked me. Since we never even kissed, there is no real bad blood or resentment or anger. Well, maybe just a little. After he went back to his wife, he told me in an e-mail, "I was thinking that what happened between us was 'just a flirtation,' but I knew it was really more than that."

Chapter 21

The Great Love—
Again and Again and Again
(2008, 2016, 2019)

"I never stopped loving you," said Alan in a Facebook message,
followed by heart and smiley face emojis.
The beginning of another try, forty-one years after we broke up.

When Alan and I broke up in 1975, he drove me all the way from Florida back home to Massachusetts. He couldn't wait for me to be out of the apartment so he could marry Peggy.

Fast forward a few decades. I never lost track of Alan. I had looked him up on the internet and knew he was still in the same area of Florida, although he had bought a house. I never contacted him until 2008 when I sent him a card for his 60th birthday. I didn't know his marital status or anything; I figured he might still be married to Peggy.

He answered with a card and a long note written in it. He was thrilled and surprised to hear from me. He had been married for over 20 years to his second wife (well, I guess Peggy didn't work out in the long-term after all, but he didn't say anything about her). He explained the marriage as "ups and downs, mostly downs"—of course. He gave me his e-mail address and asked me to stay in touch.

Less than two months later, my daughter was going to be performing in Florida—she was a skater with Disney on Ice. My long-time friend, who lived in Florida, was going to meet me for the weekend. We would stay in a hotel and see my daughter. I told Alan I would be coming to Florida, a couple of hours from where he lived. He suggested that perhaps we could meet up.

As the time got near, Alan said he would try to make it, but he wasn't sure because his wife—who he told me had medical issues she didn't take very good care of—had just been injured in an auto accident. He did manage to make it, on his motorcycle, although he was quite late, and my friend had to leave without meeting him.

Alan and I went out for lunch and walked around. I told him it was "surreal" to see him after thirty-three years. We held hands as we walked around, and I told him I felt weird because he was married. Nothing else happened, but we then continued to talk on social media and e-mail for a few months. He once told me he wished I were there with him, and then apologized for thinking that since he had a wife. And then he disappeared.

Suddenly I was unable to find him on social media, and he had stopped corresponding with me. As far as I knew, we were no longer connected on any social media. I actually became worried and went as far as to look up his brother. I messaged his brother to see if Alan was okay. He said he was fine and had remarried. I guess he meant remarried almost 30 years ago! I don't know if his brother even knew who I was.

Another eight years went by without any contact or word from Alan.

One day in September 2016, I was looking at my Facebook timeline, as I did multiple times every day. I saw a big photo of a woman attached to an obituary. I knew immediately by the last name that she must be Alan's wife. I was completely shocked. Not so much that she had passed away. I knew little about her. But I had no idea Alan and I were Facebook friends at all. I am quite sure in the years between 2008 and 2016, I had checked his Facebook profile, but there was nothing there that I could see, making me assume that we were no longer friends. I thought he probably wasn't using Facebook at all anymore. What was this obituary doing on my timeline? Had we been friends all along, but I just couldn't see anything he had posted? I was shocked, and I was saddened of course. He had by now been married to this woman for almost 40 years. I never did figure out how that post appeared on my timeline.

I wrote a comment of condolence under the post. I had no relationship of any kind with this man, and he had just written an obituary for his wife. Her death had been very recent.

Alan commented back with a thank you. Done. Over. In the past.

But you know me by now. I couldn't leave it alone because once I really "love" someone, my attachment, whatever kind it is, appears to be for life—especially when I don't have another love interest. I take great risks with my heart and then do something to mess it up—intentionally or unintentionally.

Alan had not occupied my mind when I was married and raising kids. In fact, there were probably many times when I thanked my lucky stars that I married whom I did rather than Alan.

Not being able to leave it alone, I did just what I did when Peter wanted to "friend" me on Facebook. I didn't just say yes; I had to send him a message. I had to prolong it. I had to start something.

I repeated my condolences in a Facebook private message. Nothing else. Just condolences. Alan answered with a nice thank you and some other harmless message. I waited a few days before saying anything else.

Frankly, I am embarrassed to say, I was envious. It appeared from the obituary, which he had written, that he adored this woman. Yes, I know. What else are you going to write in an obituary. But he had posted some photos, and many people who had known them as a couple, commented. It was clear she adored him, and it was clear that he—from appearances—loved her, despite what he had told me about that marriage. I felt that I had never gotten that kind of love and devotion from him.

Maybe I just didn't notice or appreciate it. However, I concluded that I was as different as night and day from his wives. Both of them. When I finally got married, all I wanted to do was be a stay-at-home mom; when I was with Alan, I had just graduated from college, and I wanted a career.

While my ex-husband wanted a woman with a career, or at least a job outside the home, Alan just wanted someone to be his wife, raise his children, and maybe work with him in his business. But at the time, that is not what I wanted. Both his wives were much less educated than I and probably much more appreciative of him, at least his second wife.

I felt envious that he seemed to be such a good husband to this woman. And when I did write to him, I wrote him something to that effect. I told him that I hoped it wasn't too soon to say something like this, but I couldn't help but see what a wonderful husband he seemed to be, and it frankly "broke my heart" to read his words about her.

It didn't take him long to write that he "never stopped loving me," nor did it take me long to tell him that I never stopped loving him either. All I had left of him was a book that he inscribed to me in 1974 and the card he had written to me nine years earlier.

After those messages, we didn't write very much. I would send a short Facebook message every few days, and we would correspond for a while and then stop. They were just friendly messages, nothing flirtatious about them. Then I noticed that he would "like" a bunch of my posts for a day, and then be quiet for a few days, and then would like them again. I admit that I was pleased when I saw him looking at my posts. Seeking the attention that I never received from my father? I still sometimes have a "meltdown" (sometimes a silent one or a mini one!) when I feel as if I am being ignored—by anyone.

After about a month, we were corresponding more frequently, to the point where we were messaging from early in the morning to late at night, despite the time difference of three hours. We started sending stickers and emojis like teenagers. He sent virtual coffee to me every morning, which I looked forward to when I woke up. I loved the attention.

Then it got to the point where if I didn't answer a message right away, he wondered where I was and would get upset. He asked me to let him know when I was going to be away from the phone, so he wouldn't wait for a reply. This surprised me. I assume that if you are near the phone, you answer right away, and if you aren't, you answer when you can.

I guess at that point, being recently widowed, he was needy and had a lot more free time than I did. He was missing a huge part of his life. He wasn't working because he had retired to take care of his wife. I was in my usual life of writing books and my blog, business as usual.

We were on opposite coasts, so we had not talked about meeting. However, two or three months after our communication began, on the phone on New Year's Eve, he told me some things that he thought I should know. He had an addiction problem, and his wife had died from an addiction. That was a little difficult for me to deal with, but it wasn't really a deal breaker. I talked to a few people I trusted about it. One of my friends said, "Run as far as you can," even before I told her much of anything. The story of how he jumped from one woman to another, having dumped me twice in the seventies, was all she needed to hear. Someone else said that only I knew what my deal breakers were, so right there I had my answer. I didn't really think these were deal breakers, although these issues did affect my feelings.

In April I was going to visit my daughter in Georgia. When I mentioned I would be somewhat close to him, he said it was too bad I wasn't going to be in his state. I was really annoyed by this, and said, "Well, I guess we are not going to have any type of relationship if you can't even try that much to see me when I am coming most of the way to where you are." After all, I was flying in from California.

He did finally offer to come see me where I would be. But it just wasn't a good idea anyway. His issues made it more difficult for him to travel. And because of my daughter's job, I was not able to see her very often. So when I did see her for a few days, my schedule was tailored to her schedule, and all the time I had belonged to her.

Since I hadn't seen Alan in a long time, I didn't know how it would go. And I didn't want to have to fit him in the schedule because I mainly wanted to see my daughter. I told him how I felt, and it was fine with him. He said he would meet my daughter another time.

And then the trouble began. I was never a very political person—at least I never thought of myself that way—although you might say I am opinionated. Well, it was 2017, and lots of people became political. I lived in liberal California, and I am from liberal Massachusetts, and even if I were from someplace else, I would be a liberal. I always was. And I don't really know anyone who isn't, partly because of where I lived and partly because my friends think the way I do.

I posted a lot of political things on Facebook, and I still do. Many people don't because of business reasons. If I were still a teacher, I would have to restrain myself. Perhaps I should restrain myself anyway because I run a small business. But I don't restrain myself on my personal social media.

One day, shortly after I returned from that trip to see my daughter, I posted a funny cartoon that was in agreement with my political beliefs. I liked it so much, it was the second time I posted it. Actually, I shared it from someone else both times.

I received a message (so it was private, not public) from Alan calling my post "disrespectful" and "unpatriotic." He stated he needed to "wash his eyes out with bleach" when he saw it. I was aghast! I had no idea Alan was "on the other side." After all, I don't hang out with anyone who feels that way. When I read his message, I was on my way out the door to have lunch with friends. I simply sent a quick message saying, "I'm done with this." There is no way I could have a relationship with someone who thought I was being "disrespectful" or "unpatriotic," when I was being, to my mind, exactly the opposite.

Alan didn't quite understand that I meant I was permanently done with this. He tried to call once or twice, and he sent messages for maybe half a day before he gave up. I managed to ignore him for a whole week. He messaged me that he thought I was done with that conversation, not done with him.

A week later I got lonely after teaching a class one evening. I impulsively messaged him a simple "hi." Because of the time difference, he didn't get it until the following morning, and he wrote back asking if that was really from me. He thought it might somehow be spam. I said it was from me.

I thought he owed me an apology for calling my post, and therefore me, those names. When I asked for one, he said. "Well, if you didn't mean what you posted, then I'm sorry." I meant it all right! I knew then that there was no way this was ever going to work. It didn't work the first two times, back in the seventies. Maybe there was a reason for that.

We did manage to "get back together" after the political dispute, but I was pretty angry. We had a couple of phone conversations where we attempted to politely disagree, but the more he said, the worse it got. I think he had tried to hide his opinions for a while; he knew I didn't agree. He knew my political viewpoint right away from my social media posts.

Right after the insult of being unpatriotic and disrespectful, I put the few things I still had from Alan into a box and sent them to him: recent Chanukah gifts, the inscribed book I had from the seventies. I mailed it out the day before I got lonely and contacted him again.

Still beating this very dead horse, I researched online to see if you can stop a package from being delivered and have it returned to you. Yes, you could. So I did. Yes, I paid extra for this.

By the time I got it back, we were on the outs again. I stuck the box in my garage. Eventually, I put the whole thing in the recycling and before I could think about it again, it was gone.

Alan wrote me shortly thereafter. He said, "It is with a lump in my throat that I say this, but I don't think we can have any kind of relationship until Trump is out of office." He added that the door was always open, meaning I could write to him any time. I never answered that e-mail.

I blocked him from my social media, from my phone, from texting. From everything except e-mail because crazy me never wants to shut all the doors. From time to time I would unblock him. Since we have a social media friend in common, whom I introduced him to, I can see if he comments on her posts, and it always bothers me to see him on there at all. So I block him again. I knew from Facebook that he had a new woman shortly after the "lump in my throat" e-mail.

The last gasp of this relationship was in 2019. Still unable to let him go, I wished him a happy birthday in July of 2019. He sent a couple of photos, and his girlfriend wasn't in them. Ever attached to him, whether or not I actually wanted to be with him, I asked if she was taking the pictures. He said, no, they had broken up.

Two months later I moved from California to Florida, where he lives, although we are on opposite coasts of Florida. The move had nothing to do with him. We weren't really communicating very much at this point. We still had that big political chasm. He did know I was in Florida, and he said he would have asked me out, but he was waiting until the political situation changed. My thought was that the external political situation could change, but our opinions still would be the same.

My good friend in Florida lives about an hour away from Alan, much closer than I do. I went to visit her for a weekend in the fall of 2019 and made a sudden decision to stop at Alan's house on my way home. He had lived there for decades, but of course I had never been there. I did call to let him know I was coming.

I figured he would have a pretty nice house, and he might clean it in preparation for my sudden visit. I was pretty shocked. The carpet was trashed with cigarette stains and holes (late wife, son?) and the house smelled of something—perhaps a mixture of cat box and cigarette smoke. I didn't say anything. His neighborhood was old and kind of rural for me. We went to some little breakfast shack that couldn't even make decent scrambled eggs and then went for a walk. But he did pick the only rose growing on his bush and give it to me as I left.

We started to talk on the phone again, and a couple of weeks after my visit, he said he would come visit me for a couple of days, probably on

Saturday. Then I didn't hear anything from him, so I didn't know if he was coming or not. I was looking for a house to buy at the time, so I made plans to look at some houses the day after he said he was going to visit. He finally called on Friday to say he was coming on Sunday. No explanation of why the day changed. So I brought him along to look at houses.

This whole thing had worn itself out long ago. I was annoyed at our differences. He had become a redneck. After we looked at a few houses, he took me to dinner at some chain restaurant he raved about. Not impressed. I wasn't feeling it, but still I wanted him.

We went back to where I was living, and he announced he was going home. I guess he decided he didn't like me enough to stay, as he had planned. I was insulted, although I wasn't interested past my lack of a relationship, my romantic notions of us decades past, and my strange attachment to him. He then said, "There is no sparkle. I wish there was, but there isn't." At that point, I should have just told him to leave. Right then. I didn't.

I loved how he was in 1973. That is how I still thought about him. But that wasn't him now. A very dead horse. I wrote him a nasty e-mail, telling him what I thought about his house.

But I still didn't stop trolling him. I continued to block him and unblock him. I unblocked him a couple of weeks ago and discovered he is engaged. Someone else who is nothing like me. I e-mailed to "congratulate" him, telling him I always thought we would end up together, but since he has married three women who aren't me . . .

I found out about this engagement a few months ago. At first it seemed to *finally* be the last nail in that coffin. My feelings seemed to finally be gone. But I feel them creeping in again. I know it is partly because I am not with anyone—nor have I been in what seems like forever. Ask me how I feel on any day, and it is different from the day before. I often think that basically he is a nice guy, and at this age, I probably should have overlooked a few things and accepted him as he is. I guess I still blame myself for the whole mess—all the decades of it. Who knows?

They say you never get over your first love.
But, sometimes . . .
You just can't go home again . . .

Epilogue

"You are smart and beautiful. Your time will come."
One of my male friends said those words to me recently.

It is 2021. It is difficult to meet anyone during a pandemic. I did meet someone at a virtual event, and we took a couple of walks together. He was perfect on paper, but there was no spark. And even though it has never worked for me, I tried online dating once again several months ago.

"Hope springs eternal." Isn't that what they say? But they also say, "If you keep doing the same thing over and over again, you are going to get the same results."

To tell you the truth, I haven't felt a spark with anyone since Noah in 2002. I used to be really depressed if there was no man in sight, even if it was someone I was meeting for coffee. I would at least have hope of finding love. I don't care as much anymore. I am used to it.

But I do hold out some hope that someday love happens for me. I don't quite know why it has been so difficult for me. But at my age, it is kind of ridiculous to keep blaming my parents.

For someone as introspective as I am, I often feel as if I don't know myself very well at all. I should have it figured out by now. Maybe there is nothing to figure out. My daughter tells me my standards are too high. They are, especially lately, despite what you have read in this book.

As the husband of one of my friends said in his online profile a long time ago:

"Sometimes you meet a frog.
*And sometimes you **are** the frog."*

Acknowledgements

There would be no book without the many men who met me, dated me, liked me, befriended me, and the two or three who maybe even loved me. Although I have changed your names and other details, I acknowledge you all.

I thank my brilliant cover designer, Steven Novak, and page designer, Marny Parkin. These people, neither of whom I have ever met, have taken my words and made the package beautiful. Marny has been with me from the beginning of my book-writing odyssey—all eleven grammar books, a novel, and now this memoir.

Thank you to my writing and publishing families past and present: Redwood Writers, Bay Area Independent Publishers Association, Florida Authors and Publishers, Florida Writers Association, Tampa Writers Alliance, and Independent Book Publishers Association.

Thank you everyone associated with National Novel Writing Month, in which I was finally able to get the first draft of this book scribbled out—way back in 2018.

Thank you to Edie Partridge, a BFF, and Shelley Bindon, my amazing daughter, who urged me to write a book about my dating experiences. And thank you to my Beta readers who offered comments and advice on how to make this a better book: Jeannie Jusaitis, Robin Moore, Rae Rae Millard, Jude Lokitch, and Jody Kravitz. Thank you to all my social media friends who voted on which cover I should use! And a big thank you to Jim Partridge who supplied the appropriate final line of the Epilogue.

Thank you to everyone who has supported me by reading my other books, my blog, and my myriad social media posts, although they are of a different topic entirely.

I thank you all.

About the Author

Arlene Miller is also known as The Grammar Diva, the author of eleven grammar books, a self-publishing book, a novel, and now this memoir. She has been an author since 2010 when she released her first book, *The Best Little Grammar Book Ever!* In 2013, she began her weekly Grammar Diva Blog, which is still going strong.  A dozen books later—because "How many grammar books can you write?"—Miller is branching out into other genres. However, her next book will be *The Best Little Business Writing Book Ever!* planned for later this year, along with a grammar course or two.

Her books have won awards from the Bay Area Independent Publishers Association (BAIPA), Florida Authors and Publishers (FAPA), and the New York Book Festival.

A former technical writer and editor, newspaper reporter and editor, copyeditor, and English teacher, writing grammar books was a natural next step. But what genres are next? "Chick literature, the genre I most like to read," she says.

Originally from the Boston area, Miller spent twenty-six years in Northern California before moving to Florida in 2019. She has two adult children and a chihuahua. Oh, and she used to be a tap dancer and instructor.

Website: www.TheGrammarDiva.com
Facebook:
    https://www.facebook.com/A-Miller-Author-141290319371177
Twitter: https://twitter.com/TheGrammarDiva
Linked In: https://www.linkedin.com/in/arlenemillerthegrammardiva/
Instagram: The Grammar Diva
Amazon: https://www.amazon.com/~/e/B003NCQX26
Goodreads:
    https://www.goodreads.com/author/show/4054842.Arlene_Miller
e-mail: info@bigwords101.com

Made in the USA
Middletown, DE
04 June 2021